UNDERSTANDING

Beginner's Guide to Programming

***

Dr Sabry Fattah

Second Edition

Published by Sabry Fattah

Table of Contents

<u>Design</u>

<u>How to improve your coding skills?</u>

Introduction

Many people hesitate to approach programming as they see it as a complex task which needs skills not easy to attain. Some believe you have to be good at mathematics to learn programming. For others, computers seem to be an enigma difficult to understand except by experts who have spent years studying at technical institutions.

In fact, programming is a skill every person should get his hands on. It does not need you to be a math wiz to program a computer. It only needs you to be able to think logically. Knowing how to program does not mean you are a software developer; it is mainly a necessity for every person in modern life. As we use software programs for every aspect of our daily life, we need to understand how these programs are designed and developed. In this way, not only that we understand fully how to use them efficiently, but also, we know what their limitations and potentials are.

Understanding software programming can also affect our way of thinking: how we identify and describe our problems? How we analyse the problem's parts? How to devise ways to manage such problems? and what logical steps to take to reach a solution?

Someone may ask: Why to bother with programming while there are thousands of software applications and programs available, some are even free to download?

Apart from those who would learn programming to promote their career and to advance to a professional level, computer programming is very rewarding. To be able to customize a program to your needs, and to design a simple script that performs exactly the task you want, is very useful and satisfactory. If you are looking for subsiding your income with freelance online jobs in web design or data science, a good knowledge and experience in programming is essential.

This book is about computer programming using Python Programming Language. Python is a very popular language used in many academic institutions, schools, businesses, and corporations. It is known for its versatility, and ability to scale its use from the simplest programming task to the most complex and sophisticated project such as artificial intelligence.

This book is aimed at the general reader. You need to try the included code snippets given here to understand fully how they behave and how they perform their tasks. A hands-on approach is very essential in learning computer programming. After installing Python on your computer - if it is not already installed - you can try the interactive system on the windows console, which is the text-only mode window. You get to this window if you type "cmd" at the Windows search box and clicking on the black icon. If you type "python" at the prompt - provided you installed Python correctly - you will be at the Python Interactive Mode prompt. You can try some calculations here like (1234/12) and see results. This gives you a feel about simple commands in Python. If you really wish to write computer code, you have to write it in a file (script) which can be run by the Python interpreter. To test your code, write a simple text file with extension ".py" and run this file from the (cmd) console.

The scripts in this book use python on Microsoft Windows. In other operating systems such scripts can also be run with very little modifications. To write and test a script, use the editor which comes with Python installation. There is an editor bundled with Python installation known as IDLE, which is short for Integrated Development and Learning Environment. It has two main windows, the Shell window and the Editor window. In this Interface, you are also able to run the code and notice output or any errors. If you write a code in the Editor window, press function key F5 to run it. You will see another window, Shell window which will show you the result and any errors you made. This is very convenient as you can make the right changes and re-run the script by pressing F5 key to see outcome.

There is another way to run a script in Python. You can run it from the DOS console. This is the text only window you get when you run the "cmd.exe". I usually create a "cmd.exe" shortcut icon on my desktop. This shortcut can be customized to point to the directory where all trial scripts are located. So, once I open the shortcut, I get to the console window. I can type the name of the script to run, press enter, and see its output. The advantage for this approach is that you get feedback about your errors. You can thus open two windows, one for the console and the other for your editor of choice, for example Windows Notepad, where you correct your code.

There are a number of available IDLE similar to the one available in Python installation. I prefer to use an advanced text editor like Notepad++ which allows code highlighting to identify different parts of the code text. Notepad++ also has a number of plugins which allow running your code and getting the output on the same screen.

It is advisable that you type each of the examples given in this book into your editor and run them as you progress through the book, rather than copy and paste them. In this way you will learn code more quickly as you understand errors you make and correct them. The hash sign # in these examples is for comments, so you do not need to enter them into your code file. The code examples include a "print" statement to display outcome of the code given. They are only needed as a demonstration of how the code works.

There is a learning curve in the process of mastering programming. The learning curve is not very steep with Python, because it is easy to understand what exactly you are try to achieve and where are you mistakes. The following chapters will help you progress along these steps.

What is Programming?

Programming is the process of creating a set of instructions that can be used to control a computer or other device. It is used to create software applications and operating systems, as well as to control robots and other machines. Programming involves writing code in a specific language, such as Python, C++ or Java, and then compiling and running the code to produce the desired output.

Programming has been around since the invention of the first computers. Early computers used punch cards and switches to enter instructions, but as computers became more sophisticated, so did the programming languages used to create software. Today, there are many different programming languages used to create applications and systems, from high-level languages such as Java and Python to low-level languages such as assembly and machine code.

Programming is used to create a wide variety of applications and systems, from simple games and media players to complex operating systems and software applications. It is also used to control robots, drones, and other machines. Programming is a highly creative activity, allowing developers to create unique solutions to complex problems.

The process of programming involves writing code in a specific language and then compiling and running the code to produce the desired output. Programmers must also debug their code, which involves finding and fixing errors in the code. Debugging can be a time-consuming process, but it is essential for ensuring that the code runs correctly and produces the intended results.

Programming is a complex and challenging activity, and it requires knowledge of multiple programming languages and concepts. Programmers must also have a good understanding of the problem they are trying to solve in order to create the most efficient and effective solution.

Programming is an ever-evolving field, with new programming languages and concepts being created all the time. As technology advances, so too does programming, allowing developers to create more powerful and efficient applications and systems.

The aim of a computer program is to solve a problem. From a simple mathematical problem such as: "How many even numbers in a series of numbers?" to a more complex one, e.g. "How to recognize the faces of people in photos?".

Programs consist of a series of instructions to tell a computer exactly what to do and how to do it. This is called an algorithm. An algorithm is a sequence of logical instructions to carry out a task. It is something similar to a recipe in cooking.

An algorithm may be written in plain English which could be a planning step before writing the true code. This is called a pseudo-code. Sometimes, a flow chart may be used to represent the steps in an algorithm to carry out the tasks. A pseudocode or a flow chart may be later translated into a computer program in the chosen programming language.

To program a computer, you need to communicate with the machine using a language it understands. The computer understands only machine code. You need a translator to help you get in contact with your computer. This translator is the programming language.

A programming language is an artificial languages that communicate with the computer structure to control its output. Any such language is made up of series of statements that give instructions to tell a computer what to do.

Programming languages are designed to be easy for a human to understand, read and write. However, a computer cannot run programs written in these languages directly. Most programming languages have to be translated into machine code before the computer can execute the instructions.

There are many different programming languages. They all share similar basic concepts although they differ in syntax and style. Some are more complicated and complex than others. Some are easier to understand for the human reader while others use concise, laconic and symbolic vocabulary.

Programming languages also differ in how they communicate with the computer structure, some are **compiled** and other are **interpreted**. A compiled language is a programming language which uses a compiler (translator program) to generate machine code from source code. The source code is compiled before it is run. Interpreted language uses an interpreter (step-by-step executor program) to generate machine code from source code during the running of the written code. Each type has its advantages and disadvantages.

Among the most popular languages are:

1- Python: an interpreted, high-level and general-purpose programming language

2- Java: a compiled language which is interpreted into bytecodes before being compiled

3- C++: a compiled programming language.

Learning programming in Python is important for a variety of reasons. Python is a powerful and versatile programming language that can be used for a wide range of tasks. It is relatively easy to learn and can be used to create powerful programs quickly and efficiently. Python is also open-source, meaning that it is free to use and modify, and it is supported by an active community of developers and users. Additionally, Python is well-supported by a large number of libraries and frameworks, making it easy to create complex applications. Finally, Python is used in many industries, from data science and machine learning to web development, making it a great choice for those looking to break into the tech industry.

PYTHON Programming Language

Python is an interpreted, high-level and general-purpose programming language. This means it uses an interpreter which translates each statement into machine code before it is executed. There are different interpreters for the various operating systems available. Python is already installed in Linux and UNIX systems, while it needs to be downloaded and installed in Windows.

Python was first released in 1991 by the Dutch programmer Guido van Rossum.

It is characterized by Readability: The reader can easily understand the meaning of the written code. Its syntax is similar to English language.

Python uses Indentation. This means that code blocks and statements are defined with whitespace indentation rather than semicolon or curly-bracket like other languages.

So, in C++ to print out "Hello World" you would use this code:

```
#include <iostream>
int main() {
cout << "Hello World!"; return 0;
}
```

In Python you write:

```
print("Hello World")
```

Python is concise in its syntax allowing users to express a complex task in few lines of code. As an interpreted language, the program is executed one line at a time, which makes correcting errors (debugging) easier.

Python is portable, so if you have a script or a program written in Python on Windows, for example, you can run it on a different platform such as Linux, UNIX, and Macintosh.

As free and open source software, it can be downloaded and used by everyone at no cost. It has a large community which contributes to a huge amount of modules and packages available online.

Python is Object-oriented language. Everything in Python is an object. It supports classes, inheritance and polymorphism. Object-Oriented programming languages allow writing a brief and reusable code. Objects are containers and templates. As containers they enclose functions and data. As templates, they create other objects similar to them with distinguished attributes. We will explain this further later in this book.

Python comes with a big standard library of packages and modules included. It has a vast range of external libraries for the various fields available through PIP, the Python Package Installer.

If you think that Python only run on the text-only Windows console, you are mistaken. Python has a number of GUI (Graphical User Interface) packages which allow developing programs with graphical windows, menus, clickable buttons and widgets. If you want to include other programming languages into your code, that is possible. Python can be extensible and integrated with other languages like C++ and JAVA. The code of other programming languages can be used inside Python code and Python code can be embedded in another language code.

Unlike C++ for example, Python has automatic memory management (Garbage collection) where blocks of memory which are not in use are reclaimed and cleared for further use.

Another interesting feature is Dynamic data typing. Data types are declared in some programming languages which is not the case with Python. Data type does not need to be declared here. This is known as Duck Typing based on the moto ("a bird that walks like a duck and swims like a duck and quacks like a duck, you call that bird a duck."). So, when you write the following statement, the interpreter understands that the characters inside double quotes are a string not a number and gives you an error warning for dividing a string by a number.

```
print("Hello world"/2)
```

In programming, we use flow control structures such as "if something happens then do that else do something else". We also use loops to repeat the same action "if a condition is true continue, otherwise this action stops". Statements are organized into blocks and each block can be given a name for reference and then this block of code is called by that name. This is known as Structured Programming. A block of statements may also receive data to work on (known as arguments or parameters) and this is known as Functional programming. Python supports both Structured and Functional programming. Dynamic name resolution allows late binding of method and variable names only during program execution.

A more advanced level of programming is using a program to create another program or modify a function whenever it is run. This is known as metaprogramming and metaobjects. We are not going to cover such advanced subjects in this book. Python supports metaprogramming techniques through its magic methods.

In contrast to other languages which offer more than one way to do something, Python embraces the design philosophy of "there should be one—and preferably only one—obvious way to do it". This makes Python less confusing for the newcomer to programming, and makes him focus on improving his skills with the tools under his hands,

Installing Python is generally easy. Go to Python download page at "https://www.python.org/downloads" and download the Windows installer then click on it and follow instructions on screen to fully install Python on your Windows operating system.

Many Linux and UNIX distributions include a recent Python installed on the system. During installation make "Python.exe" location in the system path. You can change the environmental variables in Windows to make Python in the system path by entering "env" to the search box and select to edit environmental variables. Also, remember to add ".py" to the "pathext" to make the ".py" extension associated with the Python.exe executable. In this way just typing the script file name will execute it by Python.

After installing Python, select the IDE editor of your choice to start coding in Python. Any text editor would do, though an editor with code highlighting makes things clearer and easier to understand.

DATA TYPES

Computer Data is any information converted into bytes for a computer to process using programs. A Byte is the unit of digital information transmission and storage in information technology. The most basic data measurement unit in programming is the bit. 1 byte consists of 8 bits and each bit has a state of on or off, i.e. 0 or 1. It represents the smallest location in the memory of a simple computer. This gives 256 different values which were used to store values or data in the earliest computers, i.e. characters, numbers and other symbols.

Modern computers use multiples of the 8bits in their architecture. So, 16 bits bytes will extend the capacity of each byte to 65536 values. Similarly, other structures can use 32- or 64-bits software.

Each byte has its memory address and location. Away from the complex subject of memory management and computer structure, we need to understand that anything processed and managed by a computer is in the form of bytes. Data is stored in the computer memory at a certain location and it can be called from that location for processing. It is essential to give a reference to such location to call that data.

In Programming, we use a name to refer to the data we use. We assign a name to a value, such as :

```
n = 12
```

So, the value 12 is allocated the name n and we can just use any operator or function on this name. For example:

```
print(n*n) #=> 144
```

n is the name of a variable; we call it a variable as it takes various values. It just represents a reference and indicates a location in memory. For Example, n can represent any value:

```
n = "Ho"
print(Ho*3) #=> "HoHoHo"
```

Data can be of different types:

1. Integer: that is a whole number without fractions; this can be negative or positive.

2. Float: that is a number with a fraction such as 12.45

3- String: a sequence of alphanumerical characters.

4- Boolean: True or False states.

Programming Languages use data containers to manage these basic data types. For example, to store a number of values together you gather them in a list.

```
List = [11,23,34,44,51,67]
```

You can access any value in this list by its position (known as index). You can also gather values in a dictionary, were each value has a key to access its value.

```
dictionary = {"name": "Adam", "Age": 24}
```

STRINGS

The first data type we will learn in Python is a string. Strings are written characters like the text of this book.

A string is a sequence of characters. It is still a list of bytes representing Unicode characters. In that way, it is mutable, i.e. can be modified like any list. You can split strings, extract part of them, combine them, search them, insert substring into them, etc.

Strings are represented by quotation, single or double quotes, or even triple quotes.

```
print("This is a string")
```

The difference between single, double and triple quotes is, among other things, that double quotes allow expression and escape characters interpolation (insertion of expressions or special characters). More about this in this chapter.

With triple quotes """ """, lines and spaces are separated (linefeeds remains intact) in a multiline string.

How to Format Strings

Formatting strings allow user to have control on how they will be represented on screen. It also allows inserting placeholders for values and expressions inside the string which will be executed when the string is processed. This is known as variable substitution. This makes it possible to create multiple copies of same piece of string in various forms. For example, when writing the same exact email to a number of people, the only change is the name of the person. You can create multiple copies of the same email with each name using this technique of "variable substitution".

There are three ways for formatting a string and inserting placeholders in it to substitute variables and expressions.

1- Formatting by the built-in Operator %

Try the following example:

```
name = "John"
print("Hello %s" % name)
```

The output will be "Hello John"

The variable name replaced the symbol %s (s stands for string).If the variable represents a string, we add s to % (%s) inside the string. If it is a float we use %.Nf where dotN is indicates the number of decimal points and f stands for float number.

```
print("%.2f" % 12.348732) #=> 12.35
```

Similarly, %i stands for integers which are numbers without a fraction.

```
print("%i" % 12.348732) #=> 12
```

You may substitute even an expression in the place of %s for example you may insert a list inside a string using range in list comprehension:

```
"%s " % [x for x in range(10)] #=> '[0, 1, 2, 3, 4, 5, 6, 7, 8, 9]
'
```

You may also insert a mathematical expression inside the string.

```
var = 100000
"%.2f " % int(var/12)#=> '8333.00 '
```

Remember: *The % followed by s for string, f for float or i for integer inside a double quoted string will be replaced by the variable or expression value separated from string by another % operator.*

Padding strings

Sometimes, we need to align a sequence of digits or characters to the right, left or center for a number of spaces. For this, you use %Nd or %Ns, where N is number of spaces, s for strings and d for digits. Default is right aligned.

```
print("%10d" % 123)
st = 'Hello World'
print("%40s" % st)
```

The number 123 will be printed 10 spaces to the right, and Hello world will be printed 40 spaces to the right.

If you want to align number or string to the left rather than the right, precede the N with a minus sign (-).

Actually, aligning here is done by padding a number of spaces (white spaces).

What if you want to pad a number with zeros (00)?

You just enter a zero before the number next to the % operator, i.e. %05. Notice that the 5 will represent the total number of digits including the number of digits in the number. So, if the number is 4 digits and you make N = 8, the number will be padded by 4 zeros.

```
"%05d" % 123    #5 is total number of digits
"%08d" % 1234  #=> '00001234'
```

So, in the above example the number 123 will be padded by 2 zeros as it contains 3 digits.

Remember: **To pad a number with zeros "%|0|(no. of zeros + its digit no.)|d" % number**

2- Formating by string format function

The **format()** function is a Python built-in function which is called on the string to format it. The string will have curly brackets as placeholders instead of %. Inside the {} are parameters to be substituted in their order from left to right. Such placeholders may be identified by numbers or even a keyword. The string with placeholder comes first then dot (.) then **format** followed by brackets containing the variable or expression to be substituted inside the string.

"{}".format(variable or expression)

```
"foo = {0}".format('bar')
```

You can use multiple variables, expressions, objects or strings arranged in order of the numbered placeholders inside the string. Instead of numbers you could use named placeholders inside the string and give their value in the bracketed parameters.

```
"{0},{1},{2}".format('foo', 'bar', 'zar')

"{first},{second},{third}".format(first ='foo', second
='bar',third ='zar')
```

Padding with format function

Similar to the % formatting, the **format()** function allows for padding a string to the right and left. Default is aligning to the left. Inside the curly brackets, and after identifying number or keyword name, enter a semicolon and then number of spaces to pad to the left:

```
print("{0:10} {1:10} {1:10}".format('foo', 'bar', 'zar'))

print("{first:10} {second:10} {third:10}".format(first='foo',
second='bar', third='zar'))
```

In the above example, each string is separated from the other by 10 spaces. In this way you could build a table with columns of data aligned together. More about this will be given later on.

Remember: **"{var1:spaces to the left} {var2:spaces to the left}".format(var1, var2)**

To indicate direction of alignment or where padding will be inserted, use "<" for left (this optional as it is the default) or ">" for the right alignment.

Remember:

Left align "{var:<span}".format(var)

Right align "{var:>span}".format(var)

```
print("{:>10},{:>10},{:>10}".format('foo', 'bar', 'zar'))
```

3- Formatting by F literal

The F literal is much easier and faster than the two previous formatting methods. It is simply done by putting f or F before a string which has {} curly brackets as placeholders. The placeholders would substitute variables, keyword arguments, expressions, functions, methods, objects or items in dictionaries or lists. This is very useful and easy to apply.

```
#substitute variables
a = "Hello"
b = "World"
print(f"{a} {b}")
# Substitute an expression
print(f"{120*400/23}")
# Substitute a function
print(f"{a.lower()} {b.title()}") #change variables by
lowercase and title functions.
# Substite a value extracted from a dictionary
D = dict(name = "Adam", Age = "23", sex = "male", salary
= "$2300") #dictionary
```

```
print(f"{D['name']}'s salary is {D['salary']}") #=> "Adam's
salary is $2300"
```

How to Search a String?

It is common to search some text for a specific word, phrase or
sentence. We call any part of a string substring. If you need to check
only if a string contains a certain substring, you can use the "IN"
literal which returns True or False. This may be useful to be sure that
the object contains the part before extracting it. For example, in
conditional statements when you want to correct a word in the text;
your statement will be to the effect that "if the word exists in the text
changes this word to another". IN is a very useful literal used also in
lists and dictionaries conditional statements.

```
s = "Hello World"

print('W' in s) #=> True

print("World" in s) #=> True
```

Remember : substring in string --> True/False

```
"lo" in "hello"#=> true

"ol" in "hello" #=> false

"h" in "hello"#=> true
```

This does not tell you exactly where lies your target substring. You
may use another function such as the **str.find()** function. It returns
the start position (offset) of that substring.

```
s = "http://Everyday the sun shines on the world.html"

print(s.find('world')) #=> 38
```

Remember: "string". find(pattern, offset, end) # offset is the starting position

```
#Check position of substring in a string
string = "http://Everyday the sun shines on the
world.html"
# create a function to tell you if a string contains a
substring
def findit(string, pattern, offset = 0, end = -1):
    r = string.find(pattern, offset, end)
    if r < 0:
        print("no matching substring")
    else:
        print("There is a matching string starting at position",
r)

findit(string,"word")
findit(string,"sun")
findit(string, "world")
```

The above example introduces the creation of a function to encapsulate multiple commands into a single object. It can be called later on by its name, to process its parameters (variables or arguments) given between brackets. This will explained more in the chapter about functions.

You may want to split the string at that certain position. Remember that a string is a list of characters. For example in the above mentioned string, you may split it after "http:// ".

```
string = "http://Everyday the sun shines on the
world.html"
s = string.find("//")
```

```
print(string[s+2:]) #split string after second / and end at
end of string

print(string[s+2:-5]) #split string after second / and end 5
places before
```

You will learn later in the book that a list can be split be operator [N1:N2], where N1 will be index of first item to start with and N2 is the index of the last item to stop at. You will also know that negative N means that counting index from end of list backward, so [-1] means end of list. Applying this to a string makes it possible to split a string between characters, provided you know the start and end position.

You can actually extract a substring from a long string if you know the first and end words or characters. First get the position of the start word, then the start of the word after end word, then split the string between both positions.

```
s = "http://Everyday the sun shines on the world.html"

start = s.find("the")

end = s.find("on", start)

print(s[start:end]) #=. 'the sun shines '
```

To get the N character in a string, use its position as the index

```
a = "abcde"
a[0]
```

Find and Replace in Strings

Find a Match

You will be able to find all substrings matching a pattern in long string using Regex. Regex stands for Regular Expression which is a sequence of characters that define the search pattern. It is a very powerful productive tool to search, find and replace strings and text. We will explain it in detail in another chapter when we talk about modules in Python. This module is called the "re" module. To use it, you must first import it into your script. Importing a module means all its functions and data are available to you during running your script.

```
import re
string = "too may cooks tried to spoil the broth"
print re.findall(r"\bt[\w]*", string)
```

findall() is a function which search for all substrings matching your pattern and return them in a list. The pattern has to be in a specific form, known as Regular Expressions. We will explain these later. Regular Expressions are characters which has special meaning to the module. For example, the above example searches for all words starting with letter t in the string provided. The Regular expressions used here are "\b" which means 'start with', "w" which means 'word' and * which means 'repeat'.

Another way to search for part of a string, if you know the initial or end parts of the substring, is to use **the startswith() and endswith() functions**. These functions work on any string or list.

Arguments for both functions include the part to look for and also where to search in the string. For example, you may specify where are the starting and end positions. The functions return True if substring or word starts with or ends with the given characters, False otherwise. The arguments given as a parameter to the function can also be a tuple of substrings, to find all matching substrings, True is returned if any element is found in the string. Here are some examples:

```
print("congratulation".startswith(("con", "c", "co"))) #True
print("congratulation".startswith("grat",3,10)) #True
(after 3d character)
print("congratulation".startswith("tion",-4))    #True (4th
character from end)
```

Remember: String.startswith(prefix[, start[, end]]) #True

String.endswith(suffix[, start[, end]]) #True

```
string = "concatenation"
string.endswith("tion")
string.endswith("tion", 1, 6)      #starts positions 1, and
ends at 6
tupl = ("ion","on","tion","n")     #Tuple to use for search
string.endswith(tupl)              #True if any element in
tuple is true
```

You can search and find all matching substrings in a document if you know what they start with or end with. For example in a document containing internet addresses among other text, you can get all addresses starting with http or https:

```
doc = """
http://pastebin.com/raw/0uJhLJ5m
Control the Sun ...
http://pastebin.com/raw/S4Hj3MPd
- Rolling Light Ball ...
http://pastebin.com/raw/b3QLgPcr
- Super Hungry Mcnoobington"""
lines = doc.split("\n") #split into words by spaces
for line in lines:
    if line.startswith("http"):
        print(line)
```

The Replace Function

The **replace()** function search for a substring and replace it with the argument given. It returns a new string while original one remains intact. For Example:

```
string= "Every day the sun shines on the world"
new_string = string.replace("Everyday", "Always,")
```

Remember : string.replace("old", "new") or String.replace(old, new[, count])

Replace() changes all occurrences of the pattern, but if you want to limit that to the first one only or for few occurrences, you may use the count argument as follows:

```
a = "hello world, Welcome to our new world, A brave new world"
no_count = a.replace('world', "Everyone")
count1 = a.replace('world', "Everyone", 1)
print(no_count)
print(count1)
```

Regex Pattern Searching

The "**re module**" provide access to regex pattern searching in any string. It is powerful and versatile with unlimited possibilities of search and replace inside a string or text documents.

Here are some examples:

```
import re  #remember to import module
text = 'hello world'
print(re.search('h(.+?)\s', text).group())  #search for first word starting with h
print(re.search('(.)\s', text).group())      #Any character followed by space
print(re.search('[aeiou]', text).group()) #first vowel in string
```

```
print(re.search('\w+', text).group())      #First word in
string
```

Search is a function in the **re module**. To call it, you add its name to
the name of the module separated by period (.). Its arguments are a
regex pattern followed by the name of the string to search. Notice
that it only returns the first occurrence of a match in the form of an
object, which has to be worked on by the function **group()** to return
the matching substring. This will be discussed more when in the
chapter on the "re module".

Find Position of substring

To find the position of first character of a substring in a long string,
we use the builtin function **index()**.It is possible to limit search for a
certain portion of the big string by indicating the start and end
position of that target segment. Here is an example:

```
S = "The quick brown fox jumps over the lazy dog"

print(S.index('fox'))      #16

print(S.index('dog'))      #40
```

Remember: String.index(substring [,start [,end]]) => integer

How to Slice a String

The above example reminds you that a string is a list of sequential
characters. All functions used with **Python lists** work on strings. A
string can be split at any index position or between any two
positions. In this way, it can be split into parts. This is useful for
example if you want to split a long text into two parts.

```
string = "too many cooks tried to spoil the broth"

print(string[4:14])  #=> many cooks
```

The **slice()** function is used for extended slicing. It helps to specify where to start, where to stop and how many characters to skip. This is particularly useful if you want to skip a known number of characters in a long string of numbers. See this example:

Syntax: string.slice(start,stop,step)

```
string = "1234567890"

slice_object = slice(0,50,2) #remove every second
character of words

print(string[slice_object]) #=>13579 (only it returns odd
numbers, skips even)
```

The **partition function** split a string into three parts: the part before the separator pattern, the separator itself and the part after it (pre,pattern, post). The separator can be any group of characters.

Syntax : String.partition(separator) -> (head, separator, tail) >

You can search for a separator in the string and return the part before it, the separator itself, and the part after it.

```
S = "The quick brown fox jumps over the lazy dog"

print(S.partition(" ")) #return a tuple

print(S.partition("fox")[0]) #=> The quick brown

print(S.partition("jumps")[2]) #=> jumps over the lazy dog
```

This function returns a tuple of three parts. You may get the part before or after separator if you add [0] or [2] after the function as in the example above. A tuple is a group of items indexed by numbers like lists. You get an item in any tuple or list by adding index in brackets after it.

Change String Properties

Make a copy

A string is a list of characters, so you may make a copy of the whole string or part of it in the same way as we do with lists.

```
S = "Hello World"
S2 = S[:] # make a copy of all characters in string
S2p = S[6:14] # make a copy of part of S
S3 = S
print(S, "=", S2, "=",S3)
print(S2p)
```

Repeat a String a number of times by multiplying it with * numbers

```
"Ho! " * 3
```

Hide the String

To hide a string multiply it with zero, this does not remove it from memory. To remove it completely and empty all characters, assign it to the variable None.

Syntax :String*0

```
"Ho! " * 0
a = "abcde"
a = None
a =
```

Count characters in a string

To get the size of a string in characters, use the **count() function**. It returns the number of non-overlapping occurrences of a substring in a string.

The **count()** function allows you to decide where to start and where to end in the string. Using it creatively, you can count the number of substrings or sequence of characters, or even special characters like linefeeds and newlines. In this way, you can count how many paragraphs in a document for example by the number of two linefeeds. Here is an example:

Syntax : S.count(sub[, start[, end]])

```
doc = """
This is paragraph number one.


This is paragraph number two.
You must end it with linefeed.


"""


print(doc.count("i"))        #=> count 'i' from start to end

print(doc.count("i", 5))     #=> count 'i' from position 5 to end

print( doc.count("i", 3, 14)) #=> count 'i' from position 3 to position 7

print(doc.count(""))         #=> count all characters including \s\n\r\f..etc.

print(doc.count('\n'))       #count number of lines.

print(doc.count('\n\n'))     #count number of paragraphs.
```

Split String into a List

If you want to split a string into segments of substrings and put these into a list as elements, use the **split() function**. The **split()** needs a separator as the first argument to specify what character(s) you would like to use to split a string. It returns a list of the words or segments in the string, split by the separator specified (the delimiter string).

If the separator is not specified or is None, any whitespace character (space, \n,\r,\f\s) is used as a separator. To specify a space enter it quoted as a separator. This split the string into words. To split a string into paragraphs use "\n\n" as separator. This returns a list of paragraphs. Empty strings are removed. Notice that the function follows the string and the separator is placed inside the brackets of the function. You can specify the maximum number of split segments which is optional.

Syntax : String.split([separator [,maxsplit]]) => list of substrings

```
doc = """
Start
This is line number one.
This is line number two.
End
"""

print(doc.split()) #returns words with newline characters
print(doc.split(" ")) #using quoted space returns words only
print(doc.split("\n")) #using newline returns lines of text
```

Reverse Order of Characters in a String

Characters in a string may be reversed left to right as in this example. The [::-1] reverse the order of a list or string backwards.

```
print("stressed"[::-1])#=> "desserts"
```

Join Strings

You can join (concatenate) two or more separate strings by the **plus sign** or just putting them next to each other. A comma between parts returns a tuple, but with the print statement the strings will be joined together adding a space between parts.

```
print("Hello from " + "Sam")
print("Hello from ""Sam")
print("Hello from ","Sam")
```

If you assign string parts to variables, you may add these to each other in the order you like. An object can be added to a string with the **plus sign** (even an expression or outcome of a code may be added to a string).

Syntax : "string"+object

```
L = ["Carol", "Karl", "Ian", "Mary"]
a = "Hello"
b = "The meeting will be today at 3:30pm. See you there"
for x in L :
    print(a+" "+x) # add space between 'Hello' and name
    print(b)
    print("Ian Mann, CEO")
```

In the above example, we send a message to multiple persons by adding the message content to each of their names (or email addresses) taken from a list and end it with a signature.

You may also join multiline strings by enclosing them in brackets:

```
lines = ("Alpha  "
"Beta "
"Gama "
```

```
"Delta ")
print(lines)
```

Notice that each separate line is quoted.

The same can be achieved by a backlash:

```
lines = "Alpha \
Beta \
Gama \
Delta "
print(lines)
```

An easier way is using triple quotes which will preserve the format of multiline strings:

```
ltr = """Dear Sirs
Thank you for your letter dated 12/12/2012 re:
Yours Sincerely,
Mr Ian Smith
"""
print(ltr)
```

How to Compare Strings

To compare strings, use the keyword "is" for complete equality in characters and length. It returns True or False. Equality can also be assessed by the "==" operator. Notice that upper and lowercase characters are not equal in comparison.

```
print(144 is 12*12) #True
print(144 == 12*12) #True
```

```
print("Hello World" == "Hello World")#True

print("Hello World" == "H"+"ello"+" "+"W"+"orld") #True,
value equal

print("Hello World" is "H"+"ello"+" "+"W"+"orld" ) #False,
not the same

L = ["abcdef" == "abcde", "abcdef" == "abcdef", "abcdef"
=="abcdefg", "abcdef" == "ABCDEF"]

for x in L:

    if x:

        print(x), "Because strings are equal in character and
length"

    else:

        print(x), "Because strings are not equal in either
character or length or both"
```

How to Change Style of Strings

Capitalize a String

To capitalize the first word in a string, use **capitalize()** function. To
capitalize every word in a string, use the **title()** function.

Syntax : String.capitalize()String.title()

```
str = "everyday the sun shines on the world"

str.title() #=> 'Everyday The Sun Shines On The World'

str.capitalize() #=> 'Everyday the sun shines on the world'
```

Swap Case

To swap uppercase for lowercase in a string, use **swapcase()**
function. It returns a copy of the string with uppercase characters
converted to lowercase and vice versa.

Syntax : S.swapcase() -> string

```
str.swapcase("Hello")#=> "hELLO"

str.swapcase("cYbEr_PuNk11")#=> "CyBeR_pUnK11"
```

Convert to Lowercase

To convert a string to lowercase use the **lower()**function. It returns a copy of the string converted to lowercase. This is useful when you want to make your search in a string case-insensitive. Making both the pattern and searched strings in lowercase before searching helps avoid missing words that are in either case.

Syntax :S.lower() -> string

```
a = "hEILO"
str.lower(a)
```

Convert to Uppercase

To convert all words in a string to uppercase, use **uppercase()** function. It returns a copy of the string converted to uppercase.

Syntax : S.upper() -> string >

```
str.upper("hEIIO")) #=> "HELLO"
```

Another way to capitalize each word in a string is to use the **capwords()** function from the **String module**.

```
import string
s = 'The quick brown fox jumped over the lazy dog.'
S = string.capwords(s)
```

```
print(S) #Capital S is different from small s in variable
names
```

Centering a String

To center a string on the console use the **center()** function with
arguments specifying the total length of string and spaces around it
(span), and also giving the padding character(default is spaces).

Syntax : String.center(span, padding character)

```
A = "hello".center(4) #=> width less than string length so
not working

B = "hello".center(80)#=> padded with spaces

C ="hello".center(80, '*') #=>padded with '*'

print(A)

print(B)

print(C)
```

Trimming Strings

Some strings may have unneeded extra spaces at its start or end. In
other cases, a text document may have too many empty lines or
many unintentional newline (\n) or new-paragraph characters (\n\n).
To edit and format such documents you need to remove the extra
spaces at start and end of lines, and also remove unneeded new-
paragraph's characters.

Before you do that, you need to mark your desired new paragraph
start points, so that you re-paragraph document by replacing these
marks, with new paragraph character after cleaning up your
document. To remove the trailing newline characters (\n,\r,\r\n) at
the end of lines, use the **rstrip()** function with the right arguments. If
no argument is given, all whitespace characters are removed (spaces
and newlines).

Syntax : string.rstrip()

```
"Whitespace " .rstrip()   #All whitespace removed

"Newline\n".rstrip())      #trailing newline \n removed

"hello\r\n".rstrip('\r')   #nothing removed, no trailing \r

"hello\n\r".rstrip('\n')   #nothing removed, no trailing \n

"Linefeed\r".rstrip('\r')  #trailing \r removed

"Nothing \n there".rstrip('\n')   #no trailing \n

"hello".rstrip("llo")              #trailing llo removed

"Multiple Linefeeds\r\n\r\n".rstrip())   #all trailing line
feeds removed

"Nothing here\r\n\r\r\n".rstrip("))       #nothing removed
```

Another way to remove characters from a string is to slice it using colon and square brackets to remove its last N characters. This also allows you to remove characters from the start or end of the string.

Syntax : string[:-N]

```
"string\r\n"[:-1]          #remove \n only

"string\n\r"[:-2]          #remove \n\r

"string.txt"[:-4]          #remove file extension

"concentration"[3:-5]      ##remove first 3 and last 5
characters
```

To remove whitespace from both ends of the string (remove leading and training whitespace), use **strip()** function. It returns a copy of the string with leading and trailing whitespace removed. If a particular character is given (not None), it removes such character or substring from both ends instead.

Syntax : S.strip([chars]) -> string or unicode

```
str.strip(" hello ")
str.strip("\tgoodbye\r\n")
string = "too many cooks tried to spoil the broth"
sub = string.strip("too many * the broth")
print(sub)          #return string without leading and
training substrings
```

Justified and Padded Strings

A string can be right or left justified and padded using the **rjust()** or
ljust() functions while giving the width and character to use for
padding as arguments to the functions. It returns right-justified or
left-justified string of the given length in width. Padding is done
using the specified fill character (default is a space). If width is
smaller than the length of characters in the string, nothing happens.

Syntax : S.rjust(width[, fillchar]) -> string

```
"hello".rjust(4) #=> 'hello'
"hello".rjust(20)#=> 'hello'
"hello".rjust(20, '*') #=> '***************hello'
```

The same is used to make a string left justified and padded. It returns
a left-justified string of length width given. Padding is done using
the specified fill character (default is a space)

Syntax : S.ljust(width[, fillchar]) -> string

```
"hello".ljust(4)   #less than string length
"hello".ljust(20)
"hello".ljust(20, '*')
```

LISTS

What is a List?

A list in Python is a sequence of data of any type or even objects arranged in order of sequence numbers, starting with 0 and ending at the number of elements in the list minus 1. So, a list of 10 items will be ordered in 0 to 9 sequences. This data type is known as an array in some other programming language. You may think of it as a two-dimensional table with sequential numbers as the first column.

0 Adam

1 Andy

2 Carol

3 Matt

Lists are flexible, as they can be manipulated, in contrast to a **set** which is fixed. So, you can add to start or end of a list, you can find a list element by its index number, insert an element at a specific position by giving the index of place to insert it. You will also be able to remove or delete an element, and get it from specific position, and so forth.

EMPTY LIST

Before adding elements to a list, you need to create an empty list. This can be done in two ways:

1. Assign an empty list to a variable like this: var = [], then and add elements to that variable.

2. Assign empty list to variable using list () function.

Types of list elements

A list may contain a sequence of numerical values. The basic way to create a list of sequential numbers is to use the range function.

```
L = list(range(10))
print(L) #=> [0,1,2,3,4,5,6,7,8,9]
```

The range function produces elements which starts with 0 and ends with the number before the number given in its argument. You can specify in the range function where to start and where to end, and even how many numbers to skip. For example, if you need a sequence of each fifth number in the range of numbers between from 100 to 200, you can use this

```
Print(list(range(100,200,5))) #=>
[100, 105, 110, 115, 120, 125, 130, 135, 140, 145, 150,
155, 160, 165, 170, 175, 180, 185, 190, 195]
```

List elements can be added in different ways, such as giving them as a sequence from a range or reading them from a file or database.

```
list = [1,2,3,4,5]
```

Elements in a list can be any object such as strings or a mix strings and numbers:

```
["one", "two", "three"]        #strings
[1, "two", 3.0]                #any object can be used
in a list
```

A list may contain other lists of dictionaries. Lists within list are known as **nested list**. A **Nested List** is similar to 3-dimensional tables.

```
data = [["Adam", "Andy", "Carol", "Matt"],[20, 23, 19,
26],["m", "m", "f", "m"]]
print(data[0][1])
```

In the above example the nested list "data" contains names in a list, followed by age then sex of a four persons. You can get the name of a particular person by giving the index of the first sub list and the index of that person in that list.

A dictionary can contain lists, each with a keyword, which is quite useful in data serialisation. Thus, a list may contain a number of dictionaries; and each dictionary contains a number of lists, and so on.

```
dict = {"names": ["Adam", "Andy", "Carol", "Matt"], "age":
[20, 23, 19, 26], "sex": ["m", "m", "f", "m"]}
print(dict["names"][1])
```

To get an element in a named list inside a dictionary, call that list-label from the items of the dictionary and give its index as in the example above.

Data Extraction from a list

The simplest way to extract an element from a list is to indicate its index or its place in the sequence. You should always remember that the index starts with 0, so element number 2 is placed in the third position.

```
list = [1, 2, 3, 4, 5, 6]
list[2]          #3
```

Also, you are able to get a group of elements in list between indices but not including last one. In the following example, you get the second element (index 1) and third (index 2), but not the fourth (index 3).

```
list = [1, 2, 3, 4, 5, 6]
list[1:3]   #=> [2, 3]
```

In a similar way, you can get all elements in a list from start of sequence but not including the index number given in the brackets.

```
list = [1, 2, 3, 4, 5, 6]
```

```
list[:4]    #=> [1, 2, 3, 4]  All elements excluding the fifth
element.
```

If you want to get all elements in list from index up to last one, start
with index of that element and end with None.

```
list = [1, 2, 3, 4, 5, 6]
list[3:]
```

If you want to get elements from start of list to a certain element
index, counting from end, precede that index with minus sign after a
colon. This will truncate the list by removing a number of elements
from its end that equals the index given.

```
list = [1, 2, 3, 4, 5, 6]
print(list[:-1])   #[1, 2, 3, 4, 5] remove last element
print(list[:-3])   #f[1, 2, 3] remove last 3 elements
```

To get elements in list in reverse you need to use two semicolons at
start of indexing by -1

```
list = [1, 2, 3, 4, 5, 6]
list[::-1] #=> [6, 5, 4, 3, 2, 1]
```

To get all elements in reverse and skip some elements, use the two
semicolons followed by number of elements to skip, as follows:

```
list = [1, 2, 3, 4, 5, 6]
list[::-1] #=> not skipping any
list[::-2] #=> [6, 4, 2] skipping every second element
list[::-3] #=> [6, 3] skipping every third element
list[::-4] #=> [6, 2] skipping every fourth element
```

SLICE A LIST

A list can be sliced and a portion of it extracted using the **slice()** function. Slice function will allow getting a slice with some elements skipped. First argument of slice function is index, second is where it ends and third is step or number of elements to skip.

```
arr = [1, 2, 3, 4, 5, 6]
arr[slice(4)] #=> [1, 2, 3, 4]
#from start up to but not including index 4 (fifth element)
arr[slice(2,4)] #=> [3, 4]
#between index 2 and 4(index 4 not included)
arr[slice(1,4,2)]#=> [2, 4]
#between index 1 and 4, step 2 (every second element in steps)
```

To get first element use 0 index, for last element use -1 index, or first n of list elements use index range starting from 0, to get a slice use start and end indices, to get elements from position to end do not give second index in a range.

```
arr = ['a', 'b', 'c', 'd', 'e', 'f']
arr[0]#=> first element
arr[-1]#=> last element
arr[0:3] #=> first 3 elements
arr[3:]#=> remaining elements after 3 dropped
arr[2:4] #=> from third to fourth element
```

Query elements in a list:

There are number of functions and keywords which allow user to examine certain properties of the list.

To get the number of elements in a list use keyword **len** (short for 'length')

```
browsers = ['Chrome', 'Firefox', 'Safari', 'Opera', 'IE']
print(len(browsers))      #=> 5
```

To check if a list is empty, just compare it to an empty list.

```
browsers = ['Chrome', 'Firefox', 'Safari', 'Opera', 'IE']
browsers == [] #=> False
```

To check if a list contains a given element use the syntax (**<item> in <list>**)

```
browsers = ['Chrome', 'Firefox', 'Safari', 'Opera', 'IE']
'IE' in browsers #=> True
```

Adding and Removing Elements from a List

To add elements to end of list, use the **append()** function.

```
L = [1, 2, 3, 4]
L.append(5) # add 5 to end of list
L.append(6) #add 6 to end of list
print(L)          #=> [1, 2, 3, 4, 5, 6]
```

You can insert an element at any position in a list by indicating the index of that position. The **insert() function** takes for its first argument the index of that position and the second argument is the object to be inserted in the list.

Syntax : insert(index, object)

```
L = [1, 2, 3, 4]
L.insert(1,2)                #insert 2 at second position =>
[1, 2, 2, 3, 4]
L.insert(3, [1,2,3,4])       #insert list at fourth position =>
[1, 2, 2, [1, 2, 3, 4], 3, 4]
print(L)
```

The Pop() and Remove() Functions

The **pop() function** has double action, it remove and return the item at index given; usually the last one (default). It is possible to pop a specific element by fiving its index as an argument,

```
L = [1, 2, 3, 4, 5, 6]
R = L.pop() # R value is 6 which is last item
S = L.pop(3) # S value is 4 removed at index 3
```

The **remove()** function removes the first occurrence of an element in a list and does not return its value. It takes away the value of the element to be removed from the list.

```
L = [1, 2, 3, 4, 3, 6]
L.remove(3) # [1, 2, 4, 3, 6] removed first matching element
```

The **del()** function removes an element at a given index in a list, also without returning its value.

```
L = [1, 2, 4, 3, 6]
del L[2] #=> [1, 2, 3, 6]  # del function removed first matching element at index 2
```

Removing Duplicates from a list

To remove duplicates from a list, convert it into a set (set remove duplicates and return unique elements only), then convert it back into a list.

```
a = list(set([ 1, 1, 2, 2, 3, 3, 4, 5 ])) #=> [1, 2, 3, 4, 5]
b = list(set(['foo', 0, None, 'bar', 7, 'baz', None])) #=> [0, 'bar', 7, 'baz', None, 'foo']
```

```
c = list(set([2, 5, 6, 556, 6, 6, 8, 9, 0, 123, 556])) #=> [0, 2,
5, 6, 8, 9, 556, 123]

d = list(set(["student","sam", "student","george",
"teacher","matz"]))
```

To get the index of given list value use the index() function.

```
L = [ "a", "b", "c"]
X= L.index("b")
print(X)   #=> 1
```

How to Iterate over list elements?

Iteration is going through the list elements one by one and performs a function on each element. You may iterate over list forward and in reverse (backwards).

The most basic process used for iteration is to print the list items, where you want to list each element of the list one by one. You may print them forward or in reverse.

```
list = [1, 2, 3, 4, 5]
for x in list :
    print(x)
words = "first second third fourth fifth sixth".split(" ")
for w in reversed(words):
    print(w)
```

The iteration is mainly used by for loop in which any function can be used to work on the items in a list one by one:

```
for element in list:
    function(element)
```

The map() function and lambda

The **map()** function helps to iterate over a list and apply a function on each element in the list. The function can be **a lambda function**. Lambda function is an anonymous function without a name and used inside another function to perform a task. It takes a number of arguments but only one expression. It created with the syntax (**lambda** *var*: process *var*) where **var** is any variable and **process** is any process.

The first argument in **map()** is the function can be a lambda function and the second is the list to be mapped.

* Map function returns modified list.

```
List = [1, 2, 3, 4, 5]
map(lambda a: 2*a, List) # iterate and double each item
```

Iteration on indices and elements in a list

Sometimes you need to get the index and value of each element in a list. This is particularly useful if you want to print a numbered table of values. There are two ways to do this:

1. Iterate over indices and elements together using the **range()** function of the length of list and print each index and item:

```
a = ['Mary', 'had', 'a', 'little', 'lamb']
for i in range(len(a)):
    print(i, a[i])
```

2. Iterate using the **enumerate()** function: This allow you to start numbering from 1 rather than 0 by adding a second argument to enumerate 1

```
a = ['Mary', 'had', 'a', 'little', 'lamb']
for i, e in enumerate(a,1):
    print(i, e)
```

Selection and Filtering elements of a list

If we need to select a group of elements in a list which match certain criteria, you can use the **"if" statement** or **regex matching. List comprehension** can make this much easier. We will explain List comprehension is a shorter syntax to create a new list from a processed list where selection or any function is applied.

```
List = [1, 2, 3, 4, 5, 6]
[x for x in List if x % 2 == 0]      #=> [2,4,6]
```

In the above example, we enclose the syntax in brackets to create a new list. There is a loop inside brackets which iterate over the original list applying conditional selection of items by if statement "if item (x)" is dividable by 2.

Selecting an element in list matching **regex** pattern require you to import the re module first. It is more versatile and handy.

```
import re
L = ["one", "two", "three", "four", "five", "six"]
N = [x for x in L if re.match("^[ft]",x)] # This gets the words starting with 'f' or ' t'
print(N) #=> ['two', 'three', 'four', 'five']
```

Compare and interact with more than one list

Dealing with two or more lists is easy in Python. You may need to compare them, join (concatenate) them, add one to end of the other or put it at the start, find elements which are common in both of them or elements which are different.

Comparing two lists for equality

```
a = [ "a", "a", "c" ]
b = [ "a", "b", "c" ]
set(a) == set(b) #=> compare unique items in each list
```

Joining two lists

To concatenate, i.e. join or combine two lists, you can simply use the **plus sign** to add one to the end of the other. You can add one to the start of the other list by putting it before the plus sign. The extend function add one list to the end of the other.

```
a = [ 1, 2, 3 ]
b = [ 4, 5 ]
a.extend(b) # a before b
b.extend(a) # b before a
a+b        # a before b
b+a        # b before a
```

Notice that the **join()** function **does not join lists** but *join elements in a list* into one *continuous string*. A **separator** *comes before the join function* which takes the list as a parameter.

Syntax : separator.join(list)

```
a = ["join", "those", "array", "elements", "with spaces"]
string = " ".join(a) #=> 'join those array elements with spaces'
print(string)
```

Finding the common and shared elements in two lists

The **intersection()** function returns the common and shared elements in two lists.

```
a = [ 1, 1, 3, 5 ]
b = [ 1, 2, 3 ]
set(a).intersection(b) #{1,3} are common in a and b
```

This can be also performed by if statement.

```
set([e for e in a if e in b]) #{1,3}
```

Sorting a list

Sorting numbers in a list is different from sorting strings. Numbers are sorted according to their value. Strings are sorted in alphabetical order, considering that small letters have higher value than capital letters (they come first). To sort elements in a descending order, use the reverse keyword argument. The **sort()** function takes parameters to refine sorting by key or in reverse.

Syntax : list.sort(cmp=None, key=None, reverse=False)

```
a = [66.25, 333, 333, 1, 1234.5]
a.sort()
print(a) #=> [1, 66.25, 333, 333, 1234.5]
list = ['A' ,'b' ,'C' , 'd', 'E', 'f']
list.sort(reverse=True)
print(list) #=> ['f', 'd', 'b', 'E', 'C', 'A']
```

The key keyword argument can take a function to evaluate elements in a list for sorting.

```
L = ['A' ,'b' ,'C' , 'd', 'E', 'f']
L.sort(key= str.upper)
print(L) #=> ['A', 'b', 'C', 'd', 'E', 'f']
```

DICTIONARY

A dictionary is a collection of data elements. Data is indexed, but unlike lists, the index is a name of a key to indicate the value. Only strings are accepted as keys. However, data elements can be any object, for example as a string, list or tuple. Dictionaries are not ordered in the sequence of their creation; they have no particular order as they are indexed by the keys. Keys can be sorted and searched or filtered. Each element in a dictionary is made of key-value pair. Values can be changed and modified. Changing a key means creating a new key-value pair. In Python dictionaries are written with curly brackets {}. In some other programming languages, dictionaries are known as associative arrays, maps or symbol tables.

Creating a Python dictionary

Dictionaries in Python can be built in various ways. To create an empty dictionary use curly brackets or dict() functions. Them you can later add key-value pairs one by one.

```
d = {}
d[key] = value #Enter key and value to add to dictionary d
```

Mapping Objects

dict() function allows mapping (creating a dictionary) of any object which has key-value pairs. For example, a nested list of a list which consists of pairs of key-value.

```
nl = [["key1", 100], ["key2", 200]]
dict(nl)#=> {'key1': 100, 'key2': 200}
```

Mapping Lists/Tuples/Strings

Dictionaries can be built from a list of tuples, each containing pairs of strings or string-value pairs. The list is used as an argument for the **dict()** function.

```
dict([("a", "first"),("b", "second"),("c", "third")])
```

A comma separated nested strings of couplets joined by separator such as "-" can used as an argument for dict() function. The string is made of a sequence of couplet strings joined by separator and each couplet separated from other by comma. Such string will be converted to nested list by split each couplet and then split each couplet into two parts.

```
string = ' "a" - 100, "b" - 200 '
dict(e.split(' - ') for e in string.split(','))
```

List Indices as Keys

Any list of strings can be converted to a dictionary with indices as keys using **enumerate(list)** function.

```
list = [ "a" , 100, "b" , 200 ]
dict(enumerate(list)) #=> {0: 'a', 1: 100, 2: 'b', 3: 200}
```

Even a single list of a key followed by a value in sequence can be used as an argument for dict() function.

```
list = [ "a" , 100, "b" , 200 ]
dict(zip(*[iter(list)]*2))
```

Keyword Arguments

It is possible to create a list by entering a sequence of keyword arguments to the dict() function. In this way, you avoid adding quotes to each key entered in the dictionary. Values in those keyword arguments should be quoted if they are strings.

```
dict(sape=4139, guido=4127, jack=4098)#=> {'sape': 4139,
'jack': 4098, 'guido': 4127}
```

Dictionary Comprehension

Like list comprehension, you can create dictionaries by dictionary comprehensions, as in this example

```
{x: x**2 for x in (2, 4, 6)} #=> {2: 4, 4: 16, 6: 36}
```

Dictionary from Lists

A nested list of lists each of a key-value pair of elements can be converted into a dictionary:

```
lst = [["a", 100],["b", 200]]
dict(lst) #=> {'a': 100, 'b': 200}
music = [
["Blind Melon", "No Rain"],
["Damian Marty", "Ji Gong"]
]
dict(music) #=> {'Blind Melon': 'No Rain', 'Damian Marty':
'Ji Gong'}
```

If you have two lists, the first for the keys and the second for the values, you may be able to create a dictionary using **zip()** function which combines each element in the first list with the corresponding element in the second list while building a nested list of all elements of both lists.

```
names = ["Nick", "Alice", "Kitty"]
```

```
professions = ["Programmer", "Engineer", "Art
Therapist"]

dict(zip(names, professions)) #=>{'Nick': 'Programmer',
'Alice': 'Engineer', 'Kitty': 'Art Therapist'}
```

Mapping Iterables

Dict() function can create a new dictionary (This is known as mapping) from any iterable of sequence of pairs. For example, a list of tuple pairs as follows:

```
d = {}

list1 = [('apples', 430), ('bananas', 312), ('oranges', 525),
('pears', 217)]

for k, v in list1:
    d[k] = v
```

Searching a dictionary

A) Searching for a specific Key

To search a dictionary key, use the simple keyword (IN).

```
h = {"d": 100, "a": 200, "v": 300, "e": 400}
"d" in h #=> True
"200" in h#=> False
```

You may also use the **contains()** function: *syntax Dict.contains(key)*
This returns **True** if the dictionary has the specified key, else **False**.

B) Searching for a specific Value

To search a dictionary for a value, if you know the key, use the key to get that value.

Syntax : dict[key] #=> you get the value

If you do not know the key, search all the values, you have to iterate over all the values to get the desired key-value pair that match a specific condition.

```
#search for key or value in a dict
h = { 1 : "a", 2 : "b", 3 : "c" }
for k,v in h.items():
    if v == "b" :      #it its value is b, get the key-value pair
        print(k,v)
```

If you do not know the value you are searching for, but know something about it, you may use conditional search or **regex** searching.

For example, sometimes you know that the target value is within a range of values, more or less than a certain number. In this case you use conditional 'if' as below:

```
h = { "Adam" : 100, "Bell" : 100, "Diane" : 300, "Jerry" :
200, "Fiona" : 50 }

[(k, v) for k, v in h.items() if v > 100]           #=>
[('Diane', 300), ('Jerry', 200)]
```

This will get you more than one key-value pairs matching your criteria. The result is returned in the form of a list of tuples. The if statement may contain any condition. If can also take a regex pattern like *"if re.match(pattern, value)"* , or other functions like *"if value.startswith(pattern)"*, etc.

View dictionary contents

You may need to have an idea about the dictionary in general, like its size and number of items or list of its keys.

Number of items in a dictionary

To get the number of key-value pairs in dictionary use the **'len'** keyword :

```
h = { "d" : 100, "a" : 200, "v" : 300, "e" : 400 }
len(h)
```

Get All Keys and Values

The **keys()** function gets an object containing a list of keys. To get the keys list, use **list(Dict.keys())**

```
h = { "d" : 100, "a" : 200, "v" : 300, "e" : 400 }
list(h.keys())
```

The same can be done with values, **Dict.values()** return an object containing values:

```
h = { "d" : 100, "a" : 200, "v" : 300, "e" : 400 }
list(h.values())#=> [100, 200, 300, 400]
```

With **Dict.items()** we get a list of tuples containing each key and value in a tuple form.

```
h = { "d" : 100, "a" : 200, "v" : 300, "e" : 400 }
list(h.items())#=> [('d', 100), ('a', 200), ('v', 300), ('e', 400)]
```

Extracting Data from Dictionary

Using the get() function or Dict[key]

To get the value of a key use Dict[key] expression. This is the same as the get() function : Dict.get(key)

```
h = { "d" : 100, "a" : 200, "v" : 300, "e" : 400 }
h["v"]
h.get("v")
```

The POP function with a dictionary

The **pop()** function returns the value of the key and remove it. It has the advantage of returning a message if the key is not found:

```
D = {'sape': 4139, 'jack': 4098, 'guido': 4127}
r = D.pop('sape')
print® #=> 4139
print(D) #=> {'jack': 4098, 'guido': 4127}
r2 = D.pop('john', "No such key")
print(r2)  # No such key
```

The **Dict.popitem()** function returns both the key and value in a tuple and remove them.

ITERATE OVER DICTIONARY ITEMS

You are able to iterate over dictionary items one by one similar to lists, though you need two variables: one for the key and second for the value. The **items()** function get you all the dictionary into a list of tuples which you iterate over them one by one:

```
knights = {'gallahad': 'the pure', 'robin': 'the brave'}
for k, v in knights.items():
    print( k, v)
```

Updating the data in a Dictionary

You may update data in a dictionary by adding a new key-value pair item, remove a key-value pair or modify the value of a given item.

Sometimes, you may need to delete the whole dictionary or combine it with another.

Adding an Item to a dictionary

You add an item by simply giving a new key and its value.

```
D[key] = value
```

If the key is already in the dictionary, you will be actually modifying its value. So, if not sure, check if the key exist first by *"if key not in dictionary"*, for example:

```
D = {2: 4, 4: 16, 6: 36}
if 8 not in D:
    D[8] = 72
print(D) #=> {2: 4, 4: 16, 6: 36, 8: 72}
```

Change a Key name

There are two ways to change key names, the first is to create a new key with value of key to be changed, and then delete the old key.

```
dict = { "a" : 100, "b" : 200 }
dict["alpha"] = dict["a"]   #copy item into another with
different name
del dict["a"]               # delete original item
print(dict)                 #=> {'b': 200, 'alpha': 100}
```

The other way is similar but using the **pop()** function, which remove the value of that key and give it to the new key.

```
dict = { "a" : 100, "b" : 200 }
dict["alpha"] = dict.pop("a")
print(dict)
```

Change a value in a dictionary

To change a value in a dictionary, if you have the key name, it is as easy as giving it a new value.

```
Dict[old_value] = new_value
```

Delete a dictionary item

The **del()** function deletes the key-value pair completely from a dictionary.

```
tel = {'jack': 4098, 'sape': 4139}
del(tel['sape'])
print(tel)
```

To remove all data from a dictionary and keep the empty dictionary use the **clear()** function.

```
h = { "a": 100, "b" : 200 }
h.clear()
```

Working with more than one dictionary

A) Merging Two Dictionaries

The **update()** function merge two dictionaries and remove duplicates

```
h1 = { "a" : 100, "b" : 200 }
h2 = { "b" : 254, "c" : 300 }
h1.update(h2)
h1 #value of duplicate key from the second dictionary is
used instead.
```

Substitute contents of dictionary with another

Here you are actually writing a new dictionary in the same data slot of the first one.

```
h = { "a" : 100, "b" : 200 }
h = { "c" : 300, "d" : 400 }
h
```

Working with Nested Dictionaries

A Dictionary can have a smaller sub-dictionary or a list as value for one of its keys. A large dictionary can have many sub-dictionaries as values for each of its primary keys. This is the basis of Data Interchange format of JSON. Searching a nested dictionary is through going down consecutive keys in the hierarchy to the required key-value pair in this way:

```
Dictionary[top][Mid][Down][Last_key]
```

To get value in nested dictionaries you use the sequence of **keys** in the dictionary tree structure, for example:

```
player = {
  'babe' : {
    'hits' : 2873,
    'home_runs' : 714,
    'ops' : 474
    },
  'barry' : {
    'hits' : 2935,
    'home_runs' : 762,
```

```
    'ops' : 444
  }
}
players['babe']['home_runs'] #=> 714
```

Creating a Dictionary from CSV file

A dictionary is a data container which has very fast access time. It can be searched and updated much faster than a list among other mutable objects. This makes it suitable to store and retrieve data. Data can be stored in a file on the hard disk and transferred to a dictionary during script processing. Comma separated files are simple text files where data is organized in rows with or without headings in first row. They can be converted into a dictionary using csv module.

```
import csv
reader = csv.reader(open("test.csv", 'r')) #the file test.csv
should be created first
d = {}
for row in reader:
    k, v = row
d[k] = v
print(d)
```

SETS

A set is an unordered and unindexed collection of objects written with curly brackets similar to dictionary but without keys. There is no index or key to refer to items in a set. To access items, you loop through them or find the required value using the keyword "in".

```
fruits = {"apple", "banana", "cherry"}
for f in fruits: print(f)
print("apple" in fruits) #=> True
```

Creating Sets

To create a set from a sequence of strings, use the **set()** function.

```
fruits = set(("apple", "banana", "cherry")) # note the
double round-brackets
```

Adding elements to Sets

To add one item to a set, use **add()** function. To add a number of items, use **update()** function. To add another set to the current one, use **union()** function. You may notice in the following example that items are added without any specific order.

```
fruits = {"apple", "banana", "cherry"}
fruits.add("orange")
print(fruits)
fruits.update(["pears", "passion fruit"])
print(fruits)
summer = {"dates", "mango", "grapes"}
all_fruits = fruits.union(summer)
```

```
print(all_fruits)
```

Removing Elements from Sets

To remove an item from a set; use **remove()** or **discard()** functions. **Remove()** raises an error if item does not exist, while discard does not.

The **pop()** function can be used here too, though it removes and returns the last item in a set, but you would not know which item is it as the set is not indexed nor ordered.

To delete the whole set, use **clear()** function which will remove all items and leave an empty set. **Del()** function remove the whole set and leave no trace of it.

The main advantages of a **set** is that it is immutable, i.e. fixed and non-chargeable, and also that it does not contain duplicates. So, to remove duplicated from a list, use the **set()** function.

```
L = set([1,2,4,4,5,1,3,6,2,8,3]) #=> [1,2,4,5,3,6,8]
print(L)
basket = ['apple', 'orange', 'apple', 'pear', 'orange',
'banana']
fruit = set(basket)        # create a set without duplicates
print(fruit)
```

Finding Common Elements in Two Sets

Sometimes, two sets have items that are members of both sets. You may need to examine two sets to know which items are the same, which are different and whether one set contains another or in itself is a member of another set.

Other times you may want to remove similar items in one set from another. To get all elements that exit in both sets, use the **intersection()** function which return a new set of shared elements.

To get all elements that are in current set but not the others, use the **difference()** function which return the difference of two or more sets as a new set.

To remove all elements in current set which are also present in another set, use the **difference_update()** function.

You may use set comprehension to test for set differences:

```
s = {x for x in 'abracadabra' if x not in 'abc'}
print(s) #=> {'r', 'd'}
```

Comparing Two Sets

One set may be part of another, to confirm this use **set1.issubset(set2)**. To verify the opposite, that this set contains the other set, use **set2.issuperset(set1).**

To confirm that the two sets have nothing in common, use **set1.isdisjoint(set2)**, i.e. the two sets have a null intersection.

You can also compare sets by using other operators like - & etc.. :

```
a = set('abracadabra')
b = set('alacazam')
c = set([1,2,3,4,5,6])
d = set([5,2,4,7,8,3,9])
print(a)
print(a - b)# letters in a but not in b
print(a | b)# letters in either a or b
print(a & b)# letters in both a and b
```

```
prin(a ^ b)# letters in a or b but not both
print(c)
print(c - d)# numbers in c but not in d
print(c | d)# numbers in either c or d
print(c & d )# numbers in both c and d
print(c ^ d )# numbers in c or d but not both
```

TUPLES

A tuple is a collection of items which is ordered and unchangeable. It is written with round brackets. It is similar to lists as each element has its index and similar to sets in that it is non-changeable.

Tuples can be created from a list of elements separated by commas and assigned to a variable name. Tuple elements can be any type of objects, so multiple lists can be converted into a tuple.

```
t = 12345, 54321, 'hello!'
v = ([1, 2, 3], [3, 2, 1])
```

You can create a nested tuple by enclosing the sub-tuples in brackets.

```
t = 12345, 54321, 'hello!'
u = t, (1, 2, 3, 4, 5)
u #==>"((12345, 54321, 'hello!'),(1, 2, 3, 4, 5))"
```

Like a list, you may access elements by indices, or loop through them using "for .. in .." loop.

```
fruits = ("apple", "banana", "cherry")
fruits[1] #=> "banana"
```

You can also check if an item exists in a tuple by "in" keyword or the length of tuple by len() function.

Adding Items to a Tuple

You cannot add items to a tuple, as it is immutable and unchangeable. However, you can create another tuple and add it to the first one. This will allow you to add more items at the start or end of the main tuple.

```
a = (1,2,3,4)
```

```
b = (5,) #notice the comma which is needed even if there
is only one element in the tuple
a+b ==> (1, 2, 3, 4, 5)
```

You can convert any list into a tuple using the **tuple()** function and vice versa, you can convert a tuple to a list then add items to it and convert it back into a tuple. So, if you want to add items to a tuple or modify them, convert it to a list; modify it and convert it back to a tuple.

Searching a Tuple

The **count()** function returns the number of times a specified value occurs in a tuple. The **index()** function searches the tuple for a specified value and returns the position of where it was found.

Unpacking a Tuple

A tuple may be unpacked into a number of variables. This is easier than assigning a number of values one by one when you have to define many variables.

```
x, y, z = (12345, 54321, 'hello!')   #sequence unpacking
print(x/y) #=> 0.227
```

ITERATORS

What are Iterators?

An iterator is an object that contains a countable number of values. These values are stored in a container. Such containers are named ITERABLES. You can traverse through these values by using an iterator, one by one.

ITERABLES are those containers such as lists, tuples, sets and dictionaries

We loop through an iterable using two internal functions: methods **iter()** and **next()** The iter() method converts any sequence to an iterator, which can be accessed using the next() function.

```
i = (1,2,3,4,5,6,7,8,9) # TUPLE
ito = iter(i)
next(ito) #1
next(ito) #2
next(ito) #3
object = iter("Hello")
L= list(object)
print(L)  #=> ['H', 'e', 'l', 'l', 'o'] #=> characters in a string
dic = {"one" : 1, "two" : 2}
D= list(iter(dic))
print(D)  #=> ['two', 'one'] #=> keys of a dictionary
```

The method **next()** keeps track of where it paused last time, and local variables and states are remembered between each call. This may be useful if you want to call the iterable items one by one, in steps, without starting again from scratch each time you go through them.

To iterate through an iterator in one go, you use a loop such as "for element in iterable:…do" loop.

```
i = (1,2,3,4,5,6,7,8,9)
for item in i:
    print(item)
```

The **for..loop** actually creates an iterator object and executes the next() method for each element in the iterable continuously.

You can also iterate through iterators or create an iterator by using the **iterable comprehension method**:

```
i = (1,2,3,4,5,6,7,8,9)
[print(x) for x in i] #==> [1, 2, 3, 4, 5, 6, 7, 8, 9] #LIST COMPREHENSION
```

Similarly, with tuples and sets, you can iterate through them. However, in the case of a tuple we get **a generator,** and in the case of sets we get a **subset,** depending on the expression we use in the iterator. A generator can be converted to a list using the **list()** function.

```
t = (1,2,3,4,5,6)  #tuple
s = {1,2,3,4,5,6}  #set
G= (x for x in t if x > 4)
print(G) #=> generator object
L = list(x for x in t if x > 4) #=> [5,6]
Print(L)
S = {x for x in s if x > 4}
print(S)  #=> {5, 6} subset
```

Generators

A generator is a function that returns an object (iterator) over which we can iterate (one value at a time).

```
def even(x):
    while(x!=0):
        if x%2==0:
            yield x
        x-=1
print(even(2))
```

The generator function named "even" returns each even number in a sequence of decreasing numbers starting from its parameter x.

To create a generator, we use a function. But to create an iterator we use the iter() and next() functions.

A generator makes use of the 'yield' keyword to return a value from the function similar to the "return" keyword. The **yield** keyword is specific to a generator function, and this does not exclude the use of "return" in the same function. A generator may have any number of yield statements.

Generators are memory-efficient, fast and compact code. It saves the states of local variables each time the yield pauses.

Generator in python is a subclass of Iterator. They are related but not the same. A generator can be created by a comprehension:

```
names = ("Carol Samuel", "Adam Smith", "john Berk")
gen = (name for name in names)
for name in gen:
    if name.startswith("C"): print(name)   #=> Carol Samuel
```

Comprehensions

Comprehensions in Python provide us with a short and concise way to construct new sequences from other sequences which have been already defined.

For example, to double numbers in a list you may use one of two ways:

```
#Method 1:
ns = [1,2,3,4,5]
for n in ns:
    print(n*2)
#method 2
[print(n*2) for n in [1,2,3,4,5]] #List Comprehension
```

Python supports the following 4 types of comprehensions:

* List Comprehensions

* Dictionary Comprehensions

* Set Comprehensions

* Generator Comprehensions

List Comprehension

List Comprehensions create new lists based on new conditions. You may apply an "if" statement, an expression, a function or lambda to the original list to get a new modified list. Basically, the format of list comprehension is :

```
new_list = [new_list_exp(var) for var in input_list if (var
satisfies this condition)]
```

For example, to filter some elements, we may use if condition :

```
L = [-4, -2, 0, 2, 4]
```

```
print([x for x in L if x >= 0]) #exclude negatives
```

To apply a function such as **abs()** to get absolute value :

```
vec = [-4, -2, 0, 2, 4]
[abs(x) for x in vec]
```

To call a method on each element in the original list, e.g. remove extra spaces:

```
freshfruit = ['banana', 'loganberry ', 'passion fruit    ']
[fruit.strip() for fruit in freshfruit]
```

To flatten a nested list:

```
vec = [[1,2,3], [4,5,6], [7,8,9]]
print([num for elem in vec for num in elem]) #=> [1, 2, 3,
4, 5, 6, 7, 8, 9]
```

You can also apply multiple functions from various modules:

```
from math import pi
[str(round(pi, i)) for i in range(1, 6)]#=> ['3.1', '3.14',
'3.142', '3.1416', '3.14159']
```

Dictionary Comprehension

Similar to List Comprehension, you may use the same concept with dictionaries. The main structure of Dictionary comprehension is as follows:

```
new_dict = {key:value for (key, value) in iterable if (key,
value satisfy this condition)}
```

For example, to double each value in a dictionary

```
dict1 = {'a': 1, 'b': 2, 'c': 3, 'd': 4, 'e': 5}
double_dict1 = {k:v*2 for (k,v) in dict1.items()}
```

```
print(double_dict1)    #=> {'a': 2, 'b': 4, 'c': 6, 'd': 8, 'e': 10}
```

To change keys in the dictionary

```
dict1_keys = {k*2:v for (k,v) in dict1.items()}
#=> {'dd': 4, 'ee': 5, 'aa': 1, 'bb': 2, 'cc': 3}
```

You can add conditionals to dictionary comprehensions

```
dict1_cond = {k:v for (k,v) in dict1.items() if v>2}
#=> {'e': 5, 'c': 3, 'd': 4}
```

You may use any number of conditions in dictionary comprehensions:

```
dict1_doubleCond = {k:v for (k,v) in dict1.items() if v>2 if
v%2 == 0} #=> {'d': 4}

dict1_tripleCond = {k:v for (k,v) in dict1.items() if v>2 if
v%2 == 0 if v%3 == 0} #=> {'f': 6}
```

It is also possible to use "if.. else" conditional:

```
dict1_tripleCond = {k:('even' if v%2==0 else 'odd') for (k,v)
in dict1.items()} #=> {'f': 'even', 'c': 'odd', 'b': 'even', 'd':
'even', 'e': 'odd', 'a': 'odd'}
```

You can use dictionary comprehensions with nested dictionaries:

```
nested_dict = {'first':{'a':1}, 'second':{'b':2}}
float_dict = {

 outer_k: {float(inner_v) for (inner_k, inner_v) in
outer_v.items()} for (outer_k, outer_v)
innested_dict.items()}#=> {'first': {1.0}, 'second': {2.0}}
```

Set Comprehension

Set comprehension is similar to list comprehensions. The only difference is that set comprehensions use curly brackets { }.

Generator Comprehensions

Generator Comprehensions are very similar to list comprehensions. The main difference between them is that generator comprehensions use circular brackets whereas list comprehensions use square brackets. Another difference is that generators don't allocate memory for the whole list but generate each value one by one which is why they are memory efficient.

FUNCTIONS

A function in Python is a named collection of statements which gets its data (variables or attributes) from arguments (parameters) given on its execution.

For example, the statement *print("Hello World")* can be made into a function :

```
def hi(name):
    print("hello", name)
```

This would allow reuse of a group of statements multiple times with different input of data each time they are executed. This flexibility and reusability saves a lot of time and effort in programming. The function is called by simply calling its name followed by () with or without parameters inside these brackets depending on how it was defined. A single function will serve one well-defined action or process. Related functions may be grouped together in a **class** or a **module**.

```
#create a function that writes the Fibonacci series :
def fib(n): # write Fibonacci series up to n
    """Print a Fibonacci series up to n."""
    a, b = 0, 1
    while a < n:
        print(a),
        a, b = b, a+b
# Now call the function we just defined:
fib(2000)
```

Function as an Object

The function may be assigned to a name which will have all its properties. The function here is an object which was assigned to a variable.

This allows for renaming the function, giving it a different alias and executing it in many different ways. Thus, a function can be passed as a parameter to another function. Let us try to rename a function and use its action with the new name:

```
def fib(n): # write Fibonacci series up to n
    """Print a Fibonacci series up to n."""
    a, b = 0, 1
    while a < n:
        print(a),
        a, b = b, a+b
print(fib) #=> <function fib at 0x000001D98CA07250>, an object
f = fib   #=> assign object to a variable named f
print(f)  #=> <function fib at 0x000001D98CA07250>, same object
print(f(100)) #=> function executed
```

The Return of Functions

The keyword **"Return"** followed by an expression or **None** is a command to exit the function. If there is an expression after "Return" it passes the result of that expression back to the caller. If there is no expression it returns **None**. Without Return statement, the function complete successfully and exit with **None** also returned.

The Return keyword can be used before function is completed when a conditional loop is used. Once the condition is met, the function exits, in the same way as 'break' keyword.

```
def find_prisoner_with_knife(prisoners):
    for prisoner in prisoners:
        if "knife" in prisoner.items:
            prisoner.move_to_inquisition()
            raise_alert()
            # no needs to check rest of the prisoners
            return
```

The **None** returned can be a useful outcome if a certain condition is confirmed. In the following example, the function checks if the person has a mother and he is human and returns that person's mother name, otherwise return **None**. In this example Return is used more than once in a conditional statement.

```
def get_mother(person):
    if is_human(person):
        return person.mother
    else:
        return None
```

Default Arguments

Arguments or **parameters** are values of data supplied to the function to process. These must have a name and given in the "def" statement. If no parameters are given, data are included inside the function, but this limits its reuse. Parameter names are the names of variables to which values will be assigned on execution of the function.

Sometimes, a default value is defined in the function, which will be used if no other value for such variable is given on execution or as a starting value for that variable.

```
def count(n=1):
    count += n*20
```

A more complex example follows. It asks user for data and return true or false. It uses default arguments for the number of attempts, gives feedback on errors and checks for the right input.

```
def ask_ok(prompt, retries=4, complaint='Yes or no, please!'):
    while True:
        ok = input('Do you really want to quit?')
        if ok in ('y', 'ye', 'yes'):
            return True
        if ok in ('n', 'no', 'nop', 'nope'):
            return False
        retries = retries - 1  #=> reduce number of attempts
        print(complaint)
        if retries < 0:
            raise IOError('Come on, only yes or no!')

ask_ok('OK to overwrite the file?', 2)
```

Default arguments can be of any type, for example it can be an empty list which accumulates the values passed to the function.

```
def f(a, List=[]):
    List.append(a)
    print(sum(List))
f(10),f(23),f(44)
```

Keyword Arguments

When calling a function, the caller may use keyword arguments instead of the order given in the original function definition. Parameters must be processed in the order of their position during the function definition. To overcome this, give them in *keyword:value* forms.

```
def parrot(voltage, state='a stiff', action='voom',
type='Norwegian Blue'):
    print("-- This parrot wouldn't", action,)
    print("if you put", voltage, "volts through it.")
    print("-- Lovely plumage, the", type)
    print("-- It's", state, "!")
print(parrot(1000) )# 1 positional argument
print(parrot(voltage=1000))# 1 keyword argument
print(parrot(voltage=1000000, action='VOOOOOM')) # 2
keyword arguments
print(parrot(action='VOOOOOM', voltage=1000000)) # 2
keyword arguments
print(parrot('a million', 'bereft of life', 'jump')) # 3
positional arguments
```

```
print(parrot('a thousand', state='pushing up the daisies'))
# 1 positional, 1 keyword
```

Dictionary and Tuples as Keyword Arguments

Instead of manually entering keyword arguments one by one as function parameters, it is possible to pack them together into a dictionary or a tuple and send them to the function in bulk. A dictionary would be unpacked using the double asterisk and tuples or lists by one asterisk. Any parameter missing from the dictionary will use its default value, if any.

```
def parrot(voltage, state='a dog', action='bark'):
    print("-- This dog wouldn't", action,)
    print("if you put", voltage, "volts through it.",)
    print("It is", state, "!")
d = {
 "voltage": "four million",
 "state": "not a wolf",
 "action" : "howls"}
parrot(**d)
args = [3000, "drugged"]
parrot(*args)
```

Lambda as unnamed function

Lambda is an anonymous very short function which has its own parameters and can be used anywhere even inside a named function. It always returns something, so there is no return statement here.

```
def make_incrementor(n):
    return lambda x: x + n  #lambda inside function
```

```
f = make_incrementor(42)

print(f(0)) #42

print(f(1)) #43
```

Lambda is particularly useful when used with built-in functions such as map, filter and reduce. The built-in function "**map**" applies lambda function to each item in the list. The built-in function" filter" selects items matching a condition set by the lambda function. The function "reduce" applies lambda to the first two items in the list, then again applies it to the result and continues in that way till last item.

```
L = [1,2,3,4,5]

squaredList = map(lambda x: x*x, L)

print(list(squaredList)) #=> [1, 4, 9, 16, 25]

L2 = [1,2,3,4,5,6,7,8,9,10]

newList = filter(lambda x: x % 2 == 0, L2)

print(list(newList)) #=> [2, 4, 6, 8, 10]
```

Lambda may be passed as an argument to another built-in function such as sort function

```
pairs = [(1, 'one'), (2, 'two'), (3, 'three'), (4, 'four')]

pairs.sort(key=lambda pair: pair[1])

print(pairs)
```

Docstrings

It is a matter of good style to use a docstring to describe purpose of a function. Such description would make it more readable. For someone who later would review the code to know what the function is about. They are similar to comments, but comments are short and used for a single expression or a statement. Comments are useful to explain tasks to be done, bugs and the general purpose of the module. Docstrings can be part of the documentation of the module or package. You can access documentation of a module by calling "**module.__doc__()**"function or the help(module) function.

We use a single or double quote for a single line docstring, but use triple quotes for multiline docstring.

```python
def my_function():
    """Short, concise summary of the object's purpose.

    (Starts with Capital letter and ends with period)

    (separated from description by blank line)

    More paragraphs describing the object's calling
conventions,

    its side effects..etc."""

    pass
print(my_function.__doc__)
```

CLASSES

Creation of a class

Class creation is the cornerstone of object-oriented programming. In this form of programming, you create a template or a model, from which you can create as many instances or objects as you like. Those newly created objects differ in content rather than structure, because they have different values for their variables.

A class is a container of methods and data.:

1. **Methods**: are the functions inside class. They are either invoked (called to action) on class name (e.g. class.method), or instance name (instance,method). There are Class Methods, and Instance Methods which we will explain later in this chapter.

2. **Variables** are also either Instance Variables; unique to each instance, or Class Variables shared by all instances.

Usually, the variables in the class are assigned to the instance variables on creation of the class object, even if they are empty. Also, a class may contain fixed data as CONSTANTS or Class Variables.

Think of a **class** as a machine which produce many products, objects or instances of the same "class". If you change the values in that machines during running, you get different products from the same template or production line.

For example, consider the class of "CARS" which has many individual models with slight variations. Another way to think of a class in biology as we have various types of animals of the same class:

```
class : mammals
species : cat
organism : my cat
```

My cat is similar to all other cats, but has individual characteristics and share the same biology as all mammals (i.e. they eat, grow, mate and die)

To create class, start by class definition:

```
class ClassName():
    pass #Pass means do nothing
```

Class Variables

Class Variable is given a value inside the class created during class creation not on Instance creation. It is accessible by any instance of the class, and is used by any method in the class. It can also be modified by assigning it a new value outside the class or inside the methods.

```
class Klass:
    v = 12345
print(Klass.v)
Klass.v = 88888   #=> new value assigned to class variable i
print(Klass.v)
```

Methods inside the Class

Functions inside a class are known as methods. You create a method inside the class as usual by:

```
def Method_Name(arguments/parameters):
    -- code ---
```

Instance Methods are called by name of instance and class methods are called on name of Class. Class methods follow @classmethod declaration on a separate line.

Instance Method

Even if a method inside a class has no arguments it must have 'self' as its first argument. Self refers to the class "itself". Instantiation of an object a means creating a class instance which occurs when the class is invoked with its required arguments.

```
class Klass():
    def func(self):
        print('hello world')
obj = Klass()  # instantiation or creating an instance obj
obj.func()     # calling the function func
```

```
class Klass():
    def hi(self, name): # second argument "name" required for method hi
        print('Hello', name)
a = Klass()   #instantiation
a.hi('Sam')        #argument "name" used with method "hi"
```

Remember:

1- To define a class method: use the "def" keyword, then name of method, then "self" followed by other arguments, and finally semicolon.

2- You must leave an empty line after each class or method.

3- All methods in a class should have "self" as its first argument.

Class Method

We are able to call a class method directly without an object (instance):

```
class Klass():
    @classmethod
    def method(cls):  #any word can be used instead of self
        print("this is a class method")

    def add(self):
        print(2 + 3)

Klass.method()
a = Klass()
a.add()
```

INSTANCE

An instance is a new different instance or object of the class. Values of the new object may be initialized (allocated a place in memory) on creation of the object.

```
class MyClass():
    def multiply(self, a, b):  allocate empty arguments a and b
        print(a*b)
obj = MyClass() # instantiation
obj.multiply(4,6) #values assigned to arguments a and b
```

Calling a class documentation

Documentation makes the code writing easier to follow, and the reader can understand the purpose of each line of the code. You can can call this documentation, by using the "__doc__()"function.

```
class MyClass():
    """A simple example class"""
obj .__doc__ #=> A simple example class
```

The __init__() method

This method is used to initialize instances of a class and assign arguments (with or without values) to them. It initializes arguments or parameters to accept their assigned values on creation of the instance. It gives these arguments an initial value or nothing, which will be modified later. The initial value can be the **"None"** value to make these arguments optional.

```
class Complex():
    def __init__(self, r, s, o= None):  #o argument is optional
        self.r = r  #argument r initialized
        self.s = s  #argument r initialized
        self.o= o  #argument o initialized
x = Complex(12,23)
y= Complex(12,23,35)   # another instance
print(x.r*x.s)  #=> 276
print(y.r*y.s*y.o)  #=> 9660
```

Instance Variables

These variables are unique in each instance. On the other hand, Class variables are shared by all object. Examine the following example:

```
class Dog:
    kind = 'canine'          # class variable shared by all
instances
    def __init__(self, name):
        self.name = name     # instance variable: unique value
in each instance
d = Dog('Fido')
e = Dog('Buddy')
d.kind              #=> canine (shared by all dogs)
e.kind              #=> canine (shared by all dogs)
d.name              #=> Fido (unique to d)
e.name              #=> Buddy (unique to e)
```

The class Dog has a class variable "kind" (canine) which is shared by two dogs(instances/objects) which have unique names (Fido and Buddy)

Superclass and Inheritance

As classes are objects that are created on execution of script code. They communicate with other classes and other objects by many ways. One way is to make one class a Superclass which gives access to its data and methods to other sub-classes. Other classes can inherit these methods and data from their ancestor Super class. To inherit from a superclass, the newly created class include the name of its ancestor in the parentheses after the class name.

```
class SuperKlass():
    def method(self):
        print("Hello World")
    def eql(self):
```

```
    a = [1,2,3,4]
    b = [1,2,3,4]
    print(a == b)
class MyClass(SuperKlass):
   pass
obj = MyClass()
obj.eql()  #=> True
obj.method()
```

MyClass inherits the methods eq() and method() from SuperKlass, even if the class itself is empty and has no data (pass means do nothing).

Create more than one object instance from a class

A class produces many instances and each instance can use all the variables and methods inside the parent class. Inside the class, the instance variable can be used inside any method, but it has to be referred to the instance "self", i.e. "self.variable_name". The "self" here refers to the instance created on running the class.

```
class Animal():
   def __init__(self, animal):
      self.animal = animal
   def species(self):
      print(self.animal, " is canine")
dog = Animal("dog")
fox = Animal("fox")
wolf = Animal("wolf")
print(dog.species())
print(fox.species())
```

```
print(wolf.species())
```

Classes can inherit methods from other classes

```
class Sclass(): #Sclass is superclass
    def m(self):
        print("Hello")
class Klass(Sclass):
    pass
obj = Klass() obj.m( ) #m method is a Sclass method
```

the class Klass here inherits from the class Sclass the method m.

```
class Mammal():
    def has_heart_beat(self):
        return True
class Dog(Mammal):
    pass
Fido = Dog()
print(Fido.has_heart_beat()) #=> True
```

The Dog class inherits from the Mammal class the fact (true) that dogs also have heart beats.

Ancestors of a class

To know the ancestors of a class (its super classes), import the "inspect" module and use the function getmro() which stands for "get members of that class".

```
import inspect
class Mammal(object):
    def has_heart_beat(self):
        return True


class Dog(Mammal):
    pass
print(inspect.getmro(Dog))
#=> (<class '__main__.Dog'>, <class
'__main__.Mammal'>, <class 'object'>)
```

How to get all instance variables in a class?

To get all instance variables in a class, use _dict_() function or vars() functions.

```
class Klass:
    def __init__(self):
        self.one = "foo"
        self.two = "bar"

obj = Klass()
print(obj.__dict__.keys())  #=> dict_keys(['one', 'two'])
print(vars(Klass()))  #=> {'one': 'foo', 'two': 'bar'}
print(vars(Klass()).keys())  #=> dict_keys(['one', 'two'])
```

Class as a record using empty class

A class is a container for data and methods that creates a number of copies or instances. Each new copy has its own unique values and attributes. In this way, a class can be used as a record or database, if we assign values to each instance and call these values later.

```
class Employee:
    pass
john = Employee()
john.name = 'John Doe'
john.dept = 'computer lab'
john.salary = 1000
print(john.__dict__)
#=> {'salary': 1000, 'dept': 'computer lab', 'name': 'John Doe'}
```

MODULES

A module in python is a file containing Python code. Such file may contain functions to group code together, classes and methods, as well as variables and data. Modules can be imported into any script file as a whole, where all its code will be available to the script. Sometimes, only a specific function or a class is imported from a module. This is an essential tactic for reuse of code in a flexible way.

IMPORT keyword

To use the attributes of a module including its classes and functions, you need to include an "import" statement anywhere in the script you are writing. It is customary to use it as the first statement in the script, or anywhere before you use its functions.

Notice that the module should be in the search path. A search path is a list of directories that the interpreter searches before importing a module. The interpreter search through the following paths in this order:

1. The current directory.

2. then searches each directory in the shell variable PYTHONPATH.

3. checks the default system environment path.

To check the search path, use the following statements:

```
import sys
print(sys.path)
```

It returns the current directory, and a number of python directory installations subdirectories such as 'site-packages' directory where all modules are located.

You can add any directory path to the python search path, this works only for the current python session.

```
import sys
sys.path.append(r'path to the needed directory')
```

To add a directory permanently to the PYTHONPATH, use set path function:

```
set PYTHONPATH = /usr/local/lib/python
```

IMPORT FROM

If you only need a specific class or function from a module, you can import only such attribute or even a number of functions.

```
from module_name import function1, function2, class1,
class2
from module_name import func as object
from module_name.class import func2
```

This does not import the entire module; it transfers the function into the global symbol table of the importing module.

It is possible to import everything from the module by "**from module_name import ***", though this is not recommended.

NAMESPACES

A namespace is a dictionary of variable names (keys) and their corresponding objects (values). Variables are names that map to classes, functions, script variables and the whole module. Each namespace has a scope. There are local and global scopes. Each function has its own local scope, even inside a class, the method has its own scope locally away from the class scope.

To access a local variable outside its function you need to declare it global, by a global statement:

```
def multiply(y):
    global var
```

```
var = 12
x = 15  #=> x is local variable
y = 20  #=> y is a global variable
print(x*y*var)


print(multiply(100)) #=> 3600
print(50*var)           #=> 600 (var is a global variable)
print(x*y)              #=>error: x and y local variables
inside function local scope
```

The globals() and locals() functions return the names in the global and local namespaces depending on the location where they are called. Inside a function, they will return the local and global scopes of this function.

MODULE DIR()

To access the names of all the modules, variables and functions that are defined in a module, use dir() function. The dir() function without arguments return the names of modules in the global scope. The argument is the name of the module, which will return all the functions in that module. Remember to import the module first before calling the dir() function to list its functions.

```
dir()
['__annotations__', '__builtins__', '__doc__', '__loader__',
'__name__', '__package__','__spec__']
```

Packages

A package is a hierarchical file directory structure that defines a single Python application. It consists of modules and sub-packages. For a package to be accessible it needs to be in the PYTHONPATH. Packages downloaded and installed are located in **'site-packages'** subdirectory in Python directory. To make a package accessible, put it there and add an empty "init.py" file to the root directory of the package.

You can import he package as a whole or any of its modules of functions.

```
import package_name
import pk.mod
from pk.mod import func
```

KEYWORDS

Python keywords are reserved words which are part of the syntax and core of python. They should not be used as names for variables or functions. Case-sensitive keywords should be used in lowercase except True, False and None.

In this chapter we explain some of the important Python keywords and how to use them.

Conditional Statements

The following keywords are used in conditional statements:

1. **for**: this iterates over elements of a sequence and return an iterator.

2. **if:** if executes a statement if it is true.

3. **elif:** executes an alternative statement if the previous one was false.

4. **else:** if all previous statements are False, execute this final one.

5. **break**: exit the loop.

6. **continue**: continue to the next step and skip this one.

7. True/False are implicitly implied.

8. **while:** loop through expression and stop when the condition is False.

The IF statements

When you have a condition, which may be True or False, you may use a conditional statement which will be executed if the expression is True.

This can be used in a loop to go through conditions and evaluate them one by one. The **if** statements go through the statements one by one until it finds one which returns a True Value and execute it and then break the conditional loop.

In the following example, the loop continues if the number is 0 but stops (break) if it is 5, so we get 1 2 3 4.

```
n = list(range(10))
for x in n:
    if x == 5: break
    elif x == 0 : continue
    else: print(x)
```

The "While" keyword also creates a loop, which break only if the condition is false. This may create a perpetual loop if the condition is always true.

```
n = 10
while n:
    print(n)
    n = n-1
```

In the above example, the **while** keyword evaluates the number to check if it is True, i.e. not 0 or None, print the number and reduce it by 1. Any object in Python is True, except False, None or Zero. "While n" means "while n is True" (i.e. not Zero or None or False).

The "and", "or", "not" Keywords

Those logical operators are used with the "if" and other conditional statements to compare expressions against given conditions.

And: executes an expression if both the operands are true

Or: executes an expression if either of the operands is true

Not: executes an expression if an operand is false

Here is an example of a website login which uses the three keywords:

```
Username = "Suresh"
Password = "Amanda234"
Email = "amandash@emails.com"
if Username == "Suresh" and Password == "Amanda234":
    print("login accepted")
if "@" not in Email or Email == "":
    print("incorrect email")
```

Other Keywords

Class and Function Keywords

1. def: function definition keyword

2. class: class definition keyword

3. return: return function result.

4. import: import module into script

5. from: import functions from module.

6. as: assign imported module or function to an object with a name.

7. global: make function variable a global variable accessible anywhere

8. nonlocal: make variable non local 9. pass : make function or class do nothing.

<u>**Comparison Keywords**</u>

1. **is**: Equality comparison where two objects are identical. "x is y" implies "x == y"

2. **in**: The operators "in" and "not in" test for membership. "x in s" evaluates to "True" if *x* is a member of *s*, and "False" otherwise.

Error Handling Keywords

In this section the following keywords are used:

1. assert

2. raise

3. try

4. except

5. finally

Your code may include errors which make interpreter stop execution and raise an error message. The following are keywords for managing such errors. This process is called Error or Exception handling. If you expect an error to occur, you may try **"try.. except"** statement. In this way, you give an alternative action or a message to the user once that particular error happens. For Example, to ensure that the user enter valid data, repeat the request and raise a message to user:

```

```

In the above example the message is repeated if there is an error, in particular value error as a number is expected. If the user enters a string, it will raise the exception and repeat the request for a valid number.

The **"try" statement** specifies the clean code or a group of statements. **The "except" clause(s)** specify one or more exception handlers. When no exception or error occurs in the "try" clause, no exception handler is executed. When an exception occurs (in the "try" suite), a search for an exception handler starts in the except clauses in turn until one is found that matches the exception.

Here is an example of handling more than one exception, an expression-less exception should be the last one:

```python
import sys

text = "   It is a sunny day   "
try:
    f = open('myfiletest.txt')  #=> no such file
except IOError as e:
    print("I/O error({0}): {1}".format(e.errno, e.strerror))
try:
    x = int(text.strip())   #=> text cannot be converted to
integer
except ValueError:
    print("Could not convert data to an integer.")
try:
    if " " in (text):
        print(int(text.strip())) #=> value error
except:
    print("Unexpected error:", sys.exc_info()[0])
```

```
raise
```

You may use "**else**" keyword in exception handling, as it is used in conditional flow control.

```
file = input("Enter file name: ")
try:
    f = open(file+".txt", 'r')
except IOError:
    print('cannot open file: ' +file)
else:
    print(file, 'has', len(f.readlines()), 'lines')
    f.close()
```

The keyword "finally" is always executed if it is added at the end of exception clauses:

```
def divide(x, y):
    try:
        result = x / y
    except ZeroDivisionError:
        print("division by zero!")
    else:
        print("result is", result)
    finally:
        print("executing successfully completed")

divide(122, 0)
```

As you have noticed, exception handling is used usually inside a function. Actually, you may define a class to handle errors:

```
class MyCustomError(Exception):
    def __init__(self, *args):
        if args:
            self.message = args[0]
        else:
            self.message = None
    def __str__(self):
        if self.message:
            return 'MyCustomError, {0} '.format(self.message)
        else:
            return 'MyCustomError has been raised'


raise MyCustomError('We have a problem')
```

Another way to ensure that code works without faults is to use **Testing**. The **"assert"** keyword may be used to test that a statement execution produces the desired outcome.

The Input-Output (IO) keywords

1. **with.. as..**

2. **yield**

3. **lambda**

4. **del**

5. **None**

The **"as"** clause is used in three situations :

1. to bind an imported module to a name in the expression **"import module"** or "from module import function/class"

```
Import module as m
```

2. to bind the exception to name in **exception handling**. "Except ValueError as v"

3. to bind a resource to a name accompanied by "with"

```
import numpy as np
with open('sample.txt') as fileObject:
    fileContents = fileObject.read()
```

The **"yield"** expressions and statements are only used when defining a *generator* function.

Lambda expressions (sometimes called lambda forms) are used to create anonymous functions.

Del: delete a target list recursively by deleting each target, from left to right.

BUILTINS

The **builtins module** is automatically loaded every time Python interpreter starts. The "Object" class is the base class for all Python objects, and it is defined in the **"buitlins"** module. All data types are defined in the module, e.g. string, integers, floats, lists, dictionaries, etc. All built-in Exceptions are also defined in this module.

There is a number of built-in functions in this module, which we use in any script without importing any other module.

There are some other components in that module as well, like:

- Built-in Constants: like True, False, None

- Built-in Types

- Truth Value Testing: if, while

- Boolean Operations: and, or, not

- Comparisons: is, is not, ==, !=, <, >

- Numeric Types: int, float, complex, and operators(+,-,divmod...etc.)

- Iterator Types

- Sequence Types: list, tuple, range

- Text Sequence Type : str

- Binary Sequence Types : bytes, bytearray, memoryview

- Set Types: set, frozenset

- Mapping Types: dict

- Other Built-in Types: module, class, function, method

- Built-in Exceptions

CLASSES in the BUILTINS module

There are a number of functions available inside classes among the functions in this essential module.

class object

This is the base class of the class hierarchy. The **__init__ function** is used when we create a class to initialize the instance variables

Syntax: __init__(self,*args,kwargs)**

The __new__ function creates and return a new object from any type.

Syntax: __new__(*args, **kwargs)

class property(object)

This class has a function to manage class attributes or properties. You can set, get or delete these attributes.

Syntax : property(fget=None, fset=None, fdel=None, doc=None)

Property attribute functions:

1. fget : function to be used for getting an attribute value

2. fset : function to be used for setting an attribute value

3. fdel : function to be used for del'ing an attribute

4. doc : docstring Typical use is to define a managed attribute x:

```
class C(object):
    def getx(self): return self._x
    def setx(self, value): self._x = value
    def delx(self): del self._x
x = property(getx, setx, delx, "I'm the 'x' property.")
```

Decorators make defining new properties or modifying existing ones easy: class C(object):

```
@property
def x(self):
    "I am the 'x' property."
    return self._x
@x.setter
def x(self, value):
    self._x = value
@x.deleter
def x(self):
del self._x
```

class range(object)

The **range() function** returns an object that produce a sequence of integers.

Syntax :

- range(stop) -> range object

- range(start, stop[, step]) -> range object

The sequence includes the start integer but exclude the stop integer, the step indicates how many items to skip.

> range(i, j) produces i, i+1, i+2, ..., j-1.

If the start is omitted it defaults to 0, and stop is omitted!

> range(4) produces 0, 1, 2, 3.

The following two functions can be used with a range object:

1. count(...) :

Syntax: range(object).count(value) -> integer

This function returns the number of occurrences of value in the range object (list)

2. index(...) :

Syntax: range(object).index(value) -> integer

This function returns the index of the value given.

class reversed(object)

Reversed() function reverse the order of a sequence. It can be used with strings as they are also lists of chracters, so:

```
reversed(stressed) #=> "desserts"
```

class set(object)

This class includes a number of functions to work with sets. These are:

1. **set()**: creates a new empty set object

2. set(iterable): creates a new set object from an iterable.

3. **add():** Adds an element to a set. This has no effect if the element is already present.

4. **clear():** Removes all elements from this set.

5. **copy():** Returns a shallow copy of a set.

6. **difference():** Returns the difference of two or more sets as a new set, i.e. all elements that are in this se,t but not the others.

7. difference_update(): Removes all elements of another set from this set.

8. discard(): Removes an element from a set if it is a member. If the element is not a member, do nothing.

9. intersection(): Returns the intersection of two sets as a new set. (i.e. all elements that are in both sets.)

10. intersection_update(): Updates a set with the intersection of itself and another.

11. isdisjoint(): Returns True if two sets have a null intersection.

12. issubset(): Reports whether another set contains this set.

13. issuperset(): Reports whether this set contains another set.

14. pop(): Removes and returns an arbitrary set element. Raises KeyError if the set is empty.

15. remove(): Removes an element from a set; it must be a member. If the element is not a member, raise a KeyError.

16. symmetric_difference(): Returns the symmetric difference of two sets as a new set. i.e. all elements that are in exactly one of the sets.

17. symmetric_difference_update(): Updates a set with the symmetric difference of itself and another.

18. union(): Returns the union of sets as a new set. i.e. all elements that are in either set.

19. update(): Updates a set with the union of itself and others.

class slice(object)

The **slice()** function creates **a slice object** which can be used to slice any object. It allows extended slicing with start/end points and steps.

Syntax :

* slice(stop)

* slice(start, stop[, step])

class staticmethod(object)

The **staticmethod() function** converts a function to be a static method. A static method does not receive an implicit first argument. To declare a static method, use this idiom:

```
class C:
    @staticmethod
    def f(arg1, arg2,):
        pass
```

It can be called either on the class (e.g. Class_name.function_name()) or on an instance (e.g. Class().func()). Both the class and the instance are ignored, and neither is passed implicitly as the first argument to the method.

class str(object)

The str class is the string builtin class. It contains a big number of functions to work with strings. We explained most of them in a previous chapter. Here we list all of them.

str(): converts any object to a string. argument : encoding(system default), and errors(strict or ignore)

capitalize(): make the first character upper case and the rest lower case.

casefold(): caseless version of string for comparisons.

center(width, fillchar=' '): Center a string in length width padded with specified fill character (default is a space).

count(): return number of occurrences of substring in string, optimal start and end arguments(S.count(sub[, start[, end]]) ? int)

encode(encoding='utf-8', errors='strict'): Encode the string using the codec registered for encoding.

endswith(): Return True if string ends with the specified suffix, optional start for beginning, end, stop positions. Suffix can also be a tuple

expandtabs(tabsize=8): expand all tab characters using 8 spaces.

find(): Return lowest index where substring is found, optional arguments start and end to slice string. Return -1 on failure.

format(): format string using substitutions from args and kwargs identified by braces ('{' and '}').

format_map(): format string using substitutions from mapping. The substitutions are identified by braces ('{' and '}').

index(): Return the lowest index in string where substring sub is found, within start:end Optional arguments.

isalnum(): Return True if the string is an alpha-numeric string, False otherwise.

isalpha(): Return True if the string is an alphabetic string, False otherwise.

isascii(): Return True if all characters in the string are ASCII, False otherwise. Empty string is ASCII too.

isdecimal(): Return True if the string is a decimal string, False otherwise.

isdigit(): Return True if the string is a digit string, False otherwise, i.e. all characters in the string are digits.

isidentifier(): Return True if the string is a valid Python identifier, False otherwise.

islower(): Return True if the string is a lowercase string, False otherwise, i.e. all cased characters in the string are lowercase.

isnumeric(): Return True if the string is a numeric string, False otherwise, i.e. all characters in the string are numeric.

isprintable(): Return True if the string is printable, False otherwise.

isspace(): Return True if the string is a whitespace string, False otherwise.

istitle(): Return True if the string is a title-cased string, False otherwise.

isupper(): Return True if the string is an uppercase string, False otherwise.

join(iterable): Concatenate any number of strings. The string is inserted in between each given string. 'sep'.join(iterable)

ljust(width, fillchar=' '): Return a left-justified string of length width, padded using the specified fill character, default is space.

lower(): Return a copy of the string converted to lowercase.

lstrip(chars=None): Return a copy of the string with leading whitespace removed or chars given removed instead.

maketrans(): Return a translation table usable for str.translate().

partition(sep): Partition the string into three parts using the given separator; the part before the sep, sep, and the part after it.

replace(old, new, count=-1): Replace all occurrences of substring old by new. count : Maximum number of occurrences to replace, default all.

rfind(): Return the highest index in string where substring sub is found, within optional start:end arguments.

rindex(): Return the highest index in string where substring sub is found, within start:end optional arguments.

rjust(width, fillchar=' '): Return a right-justified string of length width padded using the specified fill character (default is a space).

rpartition(sep): Partition the string into three parts using the given separator. The part before the sep, sep, and the part after it.

rsplit(sep=None, maxsplit=-1): Return a list of the words in the string, using sep as the delimiter string.

rstrip(chars=None): Return a copy of the string with trailing whitespace removed or chars removed instead.

split(sep=None, maxsplit=-1): Return a list of the words in the string, using sep as the delimiter string.

splitlines(keepends=False): Return a list of the lines in the string, breaking at line boundaries. Line breaks included if keepends is True.

startswith(prefix[, start[, end]]): Return True if string starts with the specified prefix, False otherwise With optional start, end.

strip(chars=None): Return a copy of the string with leading and trailing whitespace removed or chars removed instead.

swapcase(): Convert uppercase characters to lowercase and lowercase characters to uppercase.

title(): Return copy of string where words start with uppercased characters and all remaining cased characters have lower case.

translate(table): Replace each character in the string using the given translation table.

upper(): Return a copy of the string converted to uppercase.

zfill(width): Pad a numeric string with zeros on the left, to fill a field of the given width.

class super(object)

The **super() function** is used to give access to methods and properties of a parent or sibling class. The super() function returns an object that represents the parent class.

class tuple(object)

This class has the following functions to work with tuples.

1- **tuple(iterable=()):** To create a tuple from iterable. a tuple is a built-in immutable sequence.

2- If no argument is given, the constructor returns an empty tuple.

3- If iterable is specified the tuple is initialized from iterable items.

4- If the argument is a tuple, the return value is the same object.

The following two functions can also be used with tuples to count or get index of a value.

tup count(value): This returns the number of occurrences of value.

tup index(value, start=0, stop=): This returns first index of value and raises ValueError if the value is not present.

Class type(object)

The type() function returns the type of the argument object.

```
Print(type(12)) #=> <class 'int'> #=> It is an integer
```

Class zip(object)

Syntax: zip(*iterables) --> zip object

The **zip() function** maps multiple containers and returns a single iterator object of multiple tuples. The first element in iterable is mapped to first element in the other iterable, and it continues until elements are consumed as in the following example.

```
a = [1,2,3,4,5]
b = [100,200,300,400,500]
print([x for x in zip(a,b)])        #=> [(1, 100), (2, 200), (3, 300), (4, 400), (5, 500)]
```

BUILTIN FUNCTIONS

The following functions are essential for running any Python code. Some are used quite often such as **print(), input() or open() functions** and others are also very useful in various levels of writing code.

abs(x): returns the absolute value of the argument.

all(iterable) returns True if any element all values x in the iterable are True.

```
L = [12,34,22,45]
all(L) #=> True
all(L) > 0 #=> True
```

any(iterable) : returns True if any element in the iterable is True.

```
L = [12,34,22,45]
any(L) > 100 #=> False
```

ascii(obj) returns an ASCII-only representation of an object.

bin(number) returns the binary representation of an integer.

```
bin(2796202) #=>'0b1010101010101010101010'
```

breakpoint(*args, **kws)

callable(obj) returns whether the object is callable (i.e., function, classes, and instances of classes)

chr(i) returns a Unicode string of one character with ordinal i

$0 <= i <= 0x10ffff.$

Compile()

Syntax : compile(source, filename, mode, flags=0, dont_inherit=False, optimize=-1, *, _feature_version=-1)

It compiles a source into a code object that can be executed by exec() or eval(). The source code may represent a Python module, statement or expression. The filename will be used for run-time error messages. The mode must be 'exec' to compile a module, 'single' to compile a single (interactive) statement, or 'eval' to compile an expression.

delattr(obj, name) : Deletes the named attribute from the given object.

delattr(x, 'y') is equivalent to del x.y

dir() :

```
dir([object]) --> list of strings
```

If called without an argument, return the names in the current scope. Else, return an alphabetized list of names comprising (some of) the attributes of the given object, and of attributes reachable from it.

divmod(x,y) : Return the tuple (x//y, x%y). Invariant: div*y + mod == x.

eval() :

Syntax : eval(source, globals=None, locals=None)

Evaluate the given source in the context of globals() and locals(). The source may be a string representing a Python expression or a code object as returned by compile(). The globals() must be a dictionary and locals() can be any mapping, defaulting to the current globals() and locals. If only globals() is given, locals() defaults to it.

Exec() :

Syntax : exec(source, globals=None, locals=None)

It executes the given source in the context of globals() and locals(). The source may be a string representing one or more Python statements or a code object as returned by compile(). The globals() must be a dictionary and locals can be any mapping, defaulting to the current globals() and locals. If only globals() is given, locals defaults to it.

Format(): syntax : format(value, format_spec='')

Getattr()

Syntax : getattr(object, name[, default]) -> value

Get a named attribute from an object; getattr(x, 'y') is equivalent to x.y. When a default argument is given, it is returned when the attribute doesn't exist; without it, an exception is raised in that case.

globals() Return the dictionary containing the current scope's global variables.

hasattr : hasattr(obj, name)

Return whether the object has an attribute with the given name.

hash(obj) Return the hash value for the given object.

Two objects that compare equal must also have the same hash value, but the reverse is not necessarily true.

hex(number): Return the hexadecimal representation of an integer.

```
hex(12648430) #=> '0xc0ffee'
```

id(obj) : Return the identity of an object.

input(prompt)

input(prompt=None)

Read a string from standard input. The trailing newline is stripped. The prompt string, if given, is printed to standard output without a trailing newline before reading input.

isinstance(obj, class_or_tuple)

Return whether an object is an instance of a class or of a subclass thereof. A tuple, as in "isinstance(x, (A, B, …))", may be given as the target to check against. This is equivalent to "isinstance(x, A) or isinstance(x, B) or …" etc.

issubclass

Syntax : issubclass(cls, class_or_tuple)

Return whether 'cls' is a derived from another class or is the same class.

iter(...)

iter(iterable) -> iterator

iter(callable, sentinel) -> iterator

Get an iterator from an object. In the first form, the argument must supply its own iterator, or be a sequence. In the second form, the callable is called until it returns the sentinel.

len(obj)

Return the number of items in a container.

locals()

Return a dictionary containing the current scope's local variables.

max(...)

max(iterable, *[, default=obj, key=func]) -> value

max(arg1, arg2, *args, *[, key=func]) -> value

With a single iterable argument, return its biggest item. The default keyword-only argument specifies an object to return if the provided iterable is empty. With two or more arguments, return the largest argument.

min(...)

min(iterable, *[, default=obj, key=func]) -> value

min(arg1, arg2, *args, *[, key=func]) -> value

With a single iterable argument, return its smallest item. The default keyword-only argument specifies an object to return if the provided iterable is empty. With two or more arguments, return the smallest argument.

next(...)

next(iterator[, default])

Return the next item from the iterator. If default is given and the iterator is exhausted, it is returned instead of raising StopIteration.

oct(number)

Return the octal representation of an integer.

```
oct(342391) #=>'0o1234567'
```

open()

Syntax : file, mode='r', buffering=-1, encoding=None, errors=None, newline=None, closefd=True, opener=None

Open file and return a stream. Raise OSError upon failure. The 'file' is either a text or byte string giving the name (and the path if the file isn't in the current working directory) of the file to be opened or an integer file descriptor of the file to be wrapped.

The 'mode' is an optional string that specifies the mode in which the file is opened. It defaults to 'r' which means open for reading in text mode. In text mode, if encoding is not specified the encoding used is platform dependent

'r' = open for reading (default)

'w' = open for writing, truncating the file first

'x' = create a new file and open it for writing

'a' = open for writing, appending to the end of the file if it exists

'b' = binary mode

't' = text mode (default)

'+' = open a disk file for updating (reading and writing)

'U' = universal newline mode (deprecated)

ord()

Return the Unicode code point for a one-character string.

Pow()

pow(base, exp, mod=None)

print(...)

print(value,, sep=' ', end='\n', file=sys.stdout, flush=False)

Prints the values to a stream, or to sys.stdout by default. Optional keyword arguments:

* file: a file-like object (stream); defaults to the current sys.stdout.

* sep: string inserted between values, default a space.

* end: string appended after the last value, default a newline.

* flush: whether to forcibly flush the stream.

repr(obj)

repr(obj) : Return the canonical string representation of the object. For many object types, including most builtins, eval(repr(obj)) == obj.

round()

round(number, ndigits=None)

Round a number to a given precision in decimal digits.

Setattr()

setattr(obj, name, value)

Sets the named attribute on the given object to the specified value.

setattr(x, 'y', v) is equivalent to ``x.y = v''

Sorted()

*sorted(iterable, /, *, key=None, reverse=False)*

Return a new list containing all items from the iterable in ascending order. A custom key function can be supplied to customize the sort order, and the reverse flag can be set to request the result in descending order.

Sum()

sum(iterable, /, start=0) Return the sum of a 'start' value (default: 0) plus an iterable of numbers When the iterable is empty, return the start value. This function is intended specifically for use with numeric values and may reject non-numeric types.

vars()

vars([object]) -> dictionary

Without arguments, equivalent to locals(). With an argument, equivalent to object.dict.

The Regular Expressions

The Python "re" module provides support for regular expressions (RE) matching operations similar to those found in Perl programming Language.

Regular expressions are search patterns used to locate a matching part of a string. When you search a file for a specific string, you may use the exact ordinary sequence of characters. However, this simplistic regular expression is not always very useful.

If you want to find all occurrences of a specific string; you need to use a template pattern. This is where Regular Expression patterns come into action. For example, you may search for the exact word "cat" and you will get the exact word itself; wherever it lies in a document. But, if you want to search for all words starting with "cat", you may use the pattern "cat.{5}", which means any word starting with "cat" followed by five characters (.). This will return words like (category, catholic, catching, catalyst, catheter, catapult, catalyse, cataract, catechol, cathexis, cathouse, catchfly, catchups, caterers, catering, cathodes, ..etc).

FUNCTIONS in the re Module

The **re module** has a number of functions. The simplest of which is the **match()** function. It matches the regular expression pattern to the first match in a string and returns a match object.

The following are the most important **regex functions** in the **re** module:

1. **match()** matches a regular expression pattern to the beginning of a string.

2. **search()** searches a string anywhere for the presence of a pattern.

3. **findall()** finds all occurrences of a pattern in a string and returns a list.

4. **finditer()** finds all occurrences of a pattern and return an iterator yielding an object for each match.

5. **sub()** finds and replaces with a substitute string all occurrences of a pattern found in a string.

6. **split()** splits a string by the occurrences of a pattern.

7. **compile()** compiles a pattern into a Pattern object against which the above functions can be called.

The Compile Function

It is possible to create a pattern object against which to call regex functions.

```
import re

p = re.compile('\d+')  #=> get numbers of oneor more digits

string = "213 Lincon street, Floor 7, Flat 124"

m = p.match(string)  #=> <re.Match object; span=(0, 3), match='213'>

print(m[0])            #=> 213 is the first match in the object

s = p.search(string)  #=> <re.Match object; span=(0, 3), match='213'>

print(s[0])            #=>

f = p.findall(string)

print(f)               #=> ['213', '7', '124']

print([x.group() for x in p.finditer(string)])  #=> ['213', '7', '124']
```

The regex pattern can be more complex. It may cross multiline if you use triple quotes and parentheses. You must end such **eXtended** pattern with a flag re.Verbose or re.X. Extended patterns may even include comments preceded by hash #. For example :

```
charref = re.compile(r"""

&[#]                        # Start of a numeric entity
reference

(

0[0-7]+                     # Octal form

 | [0-9]+                   # Decimal form

 | x[0-9a-fA-F]+            # Hexadecimal form

)

;                           # Trailing semicolon

""", re.VERBOSE)
```

The Match Function

Syntax : match(pattern, string, flags=0)

This function tries to apply the pattern at the start of the string only, returning the first Match object, or None if no match was found. This object has multiple attributes and functions which can be accessed by calling them against that object, for example:

1. **span()**: returns 2-tuple (match.start, match.end) for location of the match.

2. **group()**: returns the match if it is the only one or a tuple of matching subgroups (in the case of the other function "search"). These matches are indexed by names or indices. The function **group()** takes the indices as an argument. So, when using match function, no arguments are needed as it returns the entire match.

3. **end(group=0):** return index of the end of the substring matched by group.

```
import re

string = "It rains cats and dogs"
m = re.match('It', string) #=> <re.Match object; span=(0, 2), match='It'>
print(m.group())#=> "It"
print(m.end()) #=> 2
print(m.start()) #=> 0
print(m.span()) #=> (0, 2)
```

The power of the **match()** function comes with grouping regex characters, where it starts from the beginning of string and search for other patterns in the rest of string.

For example, to search for both cats and dogs in the previous example, you may use search patterns contained inside brackets to form separate groups. The whole string is contained in group 0, while each other group is given a number from 1,2,3,4..etc , increasing from left to right. When group is used without a number, it returns the whole string, as in the following example.

```
import re
string = "It rains cats and dogs"
m = re.match('.*\s(.*)\sand(.*)', string)
print(m.group())    #=> 'It rains cats and dogs'
print(m.group(1)) #=> 'cats'
print(m.group(2)) #=> 'dogs'
```

The Search Function

The **search()** function searches for a match anywhere in the string not only at the beginning. However, it returns only one instance of the match even if there are more than one match. To find all the matches, use **findall()** function.

```
import re

string = "There are wild cats, domestics cats and pussy cats"

m = re.search('cats', string)

print(m.group()) #=> 'cats'
```

The Findall Function

Syntax : findall(pattern, string, flags=0)

The **findall()** function returns a list of all non-overlapping matches in the string. for example, to match any one single decimal number in the following example:

```
string = "213 Lincon street, Floor 7, Flat 8"

match = re.findall('\d', string) #=> ['2', '1', '3', '7', '8']
```

Find and Replace with re module

There is a dedicated function to find a sequence of characters matching a pattern and replace it with another.

SYNTAX: re.sub(pattern, repl, string[, count, flags])

1- pattern: Search pattern i.e. pattern by which you have to make replacements

2- repl: Replacement string

3- string: Original string

4- count: No of replacements to make (optional parameter)

You can use **backreference** to indicate part of the pattern in the replacement string. In the following example, we refer to any number of characters "\d+" with the "\\1" and replace them with the dollar signs added to their end. The pattern "\\1" is a **backreference** which consists of double backlashes and a number starting with 1.

```
import re
string = "213 Mobile, Charger 7, Case 8"
re.sub('(\d+)','\\1$', string)      #=> '213$ Mobile,
Charger 7$, Case 8$'
```

SPLITING with Regex

Regular expressions allow slicing of a string in ingenious ways. With **split()** function you may slice a string by whatever sequence of characters. You can also limit how many splits you like to get.

Syntax : split(pattern, string, maxsplit=0, flags=0)

Split divide the source string by the occurrences of the pattern, returning a list containing the resulting substrings. In this way, you may divide a document by the word "Chapter" for example or any sequence of characters.

```
import re
s= re.split('\s', "This is an example")  #split by spaces
r= re.split('are', "words are words are words") #split by
"are"
w= re.split('\W+', 'Words, words, words.') #split by words
w1= re.split('(\W+)', 'Words, words, words.') #grouping
words
c= re.split('[a-f]+', '0a3b9') #=> ['0', '3', '9'] #split by
alphabetical a to f
print(s, r, w,w1,c, sep="\n")
```

If **maxsplit** is nonzero, the text is split accordingly, and the remainder of the string is returned as the final element of the list.

```
import re
addesses = """Ross McFluff: 834.345.1254 155 Elm Street
Ronald Heathmore: 892.345.3428 436 Finley Avenue
Frank Burger: 925.541.7625 662 South Dogwood Way
Heather Albrecht: 548.326.4584 919 Park Place"""

entries = re.split("\n+", addesses)# split adddresses into entries by linefeed
print([re.split(":? ", entry, 1) for entry in entries])
#1 split only gives 2 parts
print([re.split(":? ", entry, 2) for entry in entries])
#split 2 , name from (address and phone number)
print([re.split(":? ", entry, 3) for entry in entries])
#split 3  name, address and phone number
print([re.split(":? ", entry, 4) for entry in entries])
#maxsplit 4 to split house number from street name
```

FLAGS

Some **re module** functions take flags as an optional argument. You may need to make search regardless of case (case-insensitive: I) or to extend the search beyond the end of line characters (the whole string whatever the number of lines: M).

Here are these flags:

A = **ASCII**: make \w, \W, \b, \B, \d, \D match the corresponding ASCII character rather than the whole Unicode(default)

You can use **backreference** to indicate part of the pattern in the replacement string. In the following example, we refer to any number of characters "\d+" with the "\\1" and replace them with the dollar signs added to their end. The pattern "\\1" is a **backreference** which consists of double backlashes and a number starting with 1.

```
import re

string = "213 Mobile, Charger 7, Case 8"

re.sub('(\d+)','\\1$', string)      #=> '213$ Mobile,
Charger 7$, Case 8$'
```

SPLITING with Regex

Regular expressions allow slicing of a string in ingenious ways. With **split()** function you may slice a string by whatever sequence of characters. You can also limit how many splits you like to get.

Syntax : split(pattern, string, maxsplit=0, flags=0)

Split divide the source string by the occurrences of the pattern, returning a list containing the resulting substrings. In this way, you may divide a document by the word "Chapter" for example or any sequence of characters.

```
import re

s= re.split('\s', "This is an example")  #split by spaces

r= re.split('are', "words are words are words") #split by
"are"

w= re.split('\W+', 'Words, words, words.') #split by words

w1= re.split('(\W+)', 'Words, words, words.') #grouping
words

c= re.split('[a-f]+', '0a3b9') #=> ['0', '3', '9'] #split by
alphabetical a to f

print(s, r, w,w1,c, sep="\n")
```

If **maxsplit** is nonzero, the text is split accordingly, and the remainder of the string is returned as the final element of the list.

```python
import re
addesses = """Ross McFluff: 834.345.1254 155 Elm Street

Ronald Heathmore: 892.345.3428 436 Finley Avenue

Frank Burger: 925.541.7625 662 South Dogwood Way

Heather Albrecht: 548.326.4584 919 Park Place"""


entries = re.split("\n+", addesses)# split adddresses into entries by linefeed
print([re.split(":? ", entry, 1) for entry in entries])
#1 split only gives 2 parts
print([re.split(":? ", entry, 2) for entry in entries])
#split 2 , name from (address and phone number)
print([re.split(":? ", entry, 3) for entry in entries])
#split 3  name, address and phone number
print([re.split(":? ", entry, 4) for entry in entries])
#maxsplit 4 to split house number from street name
```

FLAGS

Some **re module** functions take flags as an optional argument. You may need to make search regardless of case (case-insensitive: I) or to extend the search beyond the end of line characters (the whole string whatever the number of lines: M).

Here are these flags:

A = ASCII: make \w, \W, \b, \B, \d, \D match the corresponding ASCII character rather than the whole Unicode(default)

I = IGNORECASE: Perform case insensitive matching.

L= LOCALE: Make \w, \W, \b, \B, dependent on the current locale.

M= MULTILINE: Extend matching to the end of the string.

Special Characters

The Regex pattern can include any normal character or symbol. However, there are a number of special characters which extend the functionality of the patten matching.

The special characters include:

1- The **Dot "."** which matches any character except a newline.

2- "**^**" which means start of the string.

3- "**$**": matches end of the string or just before the newline.

4- "*****": 0 or more (greedy) repetitions of the preceding.

5- "**+**": 1 or more (greedy) repetitions of the preceding .

6- "**?**": 0 or 1 (greedy) of the preceding, i.e. non-greedy.

7- "***?**","**+?**","**??**" : Nongreedy versions of the previous three special characters.

8- **{m,n}**: from m to n repetitions of the preceding

9- **{m,n}?** : Nongreedy version of the above.

10- "****": Either escapes special characters or signals a special sequence like backreference.

11- **[]**: Indicates a set of characters.

12- **A:** " as the first character indicates a complementing set.

13- **AB:** creates an RE that will match either A or B.

14- **(...):** the pattern inside parentheses to be retrieved or matched later.

15- **(?aiLmsux):** Set the A, I, L, M, S, U, or X flag for the RE .

16- **(?:...):** Nongrouping version of regular parentheses.

17- **(?P<name>...):** The substring matched by the group is accessible by name.

18- **(?P=name):** the text matched earlier by the group named 'name'.

19- **(?#...):** A comment; ignored.

20- **(?=...):** if ... matches next, but doesn't consume the string.

21- **(?!...):** if ... doesn't match next.

22- **(?<=...):** if preceded by ... (must be fixed length).

23- **(?<!...)** : if not preceded by ... (must be fixed length).

Matching any character

The **dot .** is special regex character used within the search pattern which stands for any character except the newline character.

```
import re
string = "It rains cats and dogs"
m = re.findall('.{3,4}s', string) #3 or 4 characters words
ending in s
print(m) #=> ['rains', ' cats', ' dogs']
```

Repetition of Characters

The asterisk character repeats the preceding character as many times as possible. This is the greedy use. To limit such behaviour, follow the asterisk with question mark "?"

The same result can be obtained by the plus sign which is more precise as it repeats the preceding characters once or more than once.

Another way of repeating the previous characters is using curly brackets with minimal and maximum repetition. So, asterisk is equal to {0,} and + is equal to {1,}

```python
import re
string = "all my mind thoughts"
m = re.search('.*', string).group() #all my mind thoughts
m1 = re.search('.+', string).group() #all my mind thoughts
m2 = re.findall('\s.{2}\s', string)
m3 = re.findall('.{,4}\s', string)
print(m)
print(m1)
print(m2) #[' my ']
print(m3) #['all ', 'my ', 'mind ']
```

To match a character or pattern at the beginning of a string use "^". In Multiline text with newline characters, use the flag Multiline or M to cross the lines.

```python
import re
text = """Ross McFluff: 834.345.1254 155 Elm Street
Ronald Heathmore: 892.345.3428 436 Finley Avenue
Frank Burger: 925.541.7625 662 South Dogwood Way
Heather Albrecht: 548.326.4584 919 Park Place"""
```

```
m = re.findall('^[R].*', text, re.M) #finds all entries starting
with capital R

print(m) #=>

['Ross McFluff: 834.345.1254 155 Elm Street', 'Ronald
Heathmore: 892.345.3428 436 Finley Avenue']
```

To match a pattern at end of string or just before the newline character use the dollar sign $

```
import re

text = """Ross McFluff: 834.345.1254 155 Elm Street

Ronald Heathmore: 892.345.3428 436 Finley Avenue

Frank Burger: 925.541.7625 662 South Dogwood Way

Heather Albrecht: 548.326.4584 919 Park Place"""

m = re.findall('.*Street$', text, re.M)  #finds entry ending
in "Street"

print(m) #=> ['Ross McFluff: 834.345.1254 155 Elm
Street']
```

Matching a Set of Characters

You may enclose a set of characters inside square brackets. Any one of the characters in that set will be matched against the string. Thus, [a-z] means any lowercase alphabetical character, [A-Z] any uppercase alphabetical character, [0-9] any number, and [a-zA-Z0-9] means any alphanumerical character and any space too.

You can use a partial set of characters and indicate range by a hyphen. If you add "^" outside the set, it will match any string starting with any character in the set. If you include the "^" inside the set it will mean the opposite: it will exclude any character in the set from matching.

```
import re

text = """Ross McFluff: 834.345.1254 155 Elm Street

Ronald Heathmore: 892.345.3428 436 Finley Avenue

Frank Burger: 925.541.7625 662 South Dogwood Way

Heather Albrecht: 548.326.4584 919 Park Place"""

m = re.findall('^[M-Z].*', text, re.M)

[print(e) for e in m]
```

Grouping sub-patterns

A group is a subexpression of the regex search pattern which is contained within parentheses. Groups are numbered from left to right starting with 1, while group 0 is the whole text matched by the entire regex expression.

1. You can **catch** one or more of the matching groups by match.group(n) function.

2. You can **catch** a group by backreference where \1 refer to group 1 and so on.

3. **A captured group** in a search pattern may be repeated by backreference in the same pattern.

```
import re

p = re.compile(r'\b(\w+)\s+\1\b') #catch repeated words
forllowed by space

m = p.search('Paris in the the spring').group()

print(m) #the the
```

Groups can be nested and here you count their number by counting the open parenthesis from left to right.

```
import re
string = "Ethnic groups in UK: Asians, Africans and Whites
groups"
m = re.search("(Asians), (.*) and (Whites)", string)
m.group()
m.group(0) #=> Asians, Africans and Whites'
m.group(1) #=> 'Asians'
m.group(2) #=> 'Africans'
m.group(3) #=> 'Whites'
```

Groups may be named and backreferenced with <name> and defined by (?P<name>pattern)

```
import re
string = "Today at 12:30 PM on London's Echo"
p = re.compile(r'(?P<day>\w+) at (?P<time>(\d+):(\d+)
(\w+)) on (?P<place>\w+)')
m = p.match(string)
print(m.groups()) #=> ('Today', '12:30 PM', '12', '30', 'PM',
'London')
print(m.group('day')) #=>'Today'
print(m.group('time'))#=> '12:30 PM'
print(m.group('place')) #=>'London'
```

```
import re
m = re.match(r"(?P<first_name>\w+)
(?P<last_name>\w+)", "Malcolm Reynolds")
```

```
print(m.group())        #Malcolm Reynolds

print(m.groupdict())    #=> {'first_name': 'Malcolm',
'last_name': 'Reynolds'}
```

Lookahead and Lookbehind

Lookahead and **Lookbehind** are known as **Lookarounds**. They are assertions that some characters come before or after the target search pattern. So, you may add more than one Lookarounds and the engine would still start matching at the pattern given. They do not consume the pattern as the engine remains at its start. Lookarounds can be positive assertion or negative assertion.

To use lookahead, add the characters following the pattern in parenthesis after "?=".

```
import re

p = re.compile(r'.\d+(?= dollars)') #catch digits before the
word "dollars"

m= p.search('It costs 123 dollars and 25 cents').group()

print(m) #=> 123
```

In the above example, the engine matches the 123 and then **asserts** that the digits at that position is followed immediately by the word dollars.

To use look behind, you may add the same assertion before the pattern.

```
import re

p = re.compile(r'.(?=\d+ cents)\d+')

m= p.search('It costs 123 dollars and 25 cents').group()

print(m)   #=> 25
```

A much better way is to use "?< =" to indicate the direction of assertion for the pattern.

```
import re

p = re.compile(r'(?<=USD)\d{3}') # 3 digits preceded by USD

m = p.search('It costs USD123 dollars and 25 cents').group()

print(m) #=> 123
```

To use negative assertion, i.e. that the pattern is not preceded or followed by the assertion given, you may use ! in the place of equal '=' sign.

```
import re

p = re.compile(r'\d{3}(?<!\scents)') #three digits not followed by "cents"

m = p.search('It costs USD123 dollars and 25 cents')

print(m.group()) #=> 123
```

Python require that a lookbehind to match a string of fixed length, so (?<cat|dogs) will not work.

Special Escape Characters

They consist of "\\" and a character.

\number = Matches the contents of the group of the same number.

\A = Matches only at the start of the string.

\Z = Matches only at the end of the string.

\b = Matches the empty string, but only at the start or end of a word.

\B = Matches the empty string, but not at the start or end of a word.

\d = Matches any decimal digit; equivalent to the set'[0-9]'

\D = Matches any non-digit character; equivalent to [caret\d]

\s = Matches any whitespace character; equivalent to '[\t\n\r\f\v]'

\S = Matches any non-whitespace character; equivalent to [caret\s].

\w = Matches any alphanumeric character; equivalent to '[a-zA-Z0-9_]'

\W = Matches the complement of \w.

\\ = Matches a literal backslash.

FILES

Printing on the Console

The **print()** function send a string object to the Standard Output device, which is usually the screen or console. Any object which can be converted to a string can be printed to the screen, so a list, dictionary, tuple, or math expression, etc. may be printed.

Print function takes a number of useful arguments:

object(s) = This is essential : Any number of objects separated by commas will be converted to strings

sep 'separator' = Thid id optional : it will clarify how objects will be separated?. Default is space' '

end.'end' = What to print at the end? Default is '\n' (line feed)

file = Optional: Where the objects will be written?. Default is sys.stdout, this can be changed to any file.

flush = Optional: Will the output be flushed? (True) or buffered (False). Default is False

So, any number of objects may be printed to console or to file, separated by spaces or commas or linefeeds, and ending in linefeed or none at all. The print() function without arguments, will give a newline after it finishes.

```
import sys


x = 12
y = 22
print("Hello World")        #remember to add brackets
print("The answer is", 2*2) #execute an operation
```

```
print(x, end=" ")                #end is empty, will join it with
next print

print(10*x, y,end="\n")     #print 2 objects x and y

print()                          #NEWLINE

print("fatal error", file=sys.stderr)   #print to standard
error

print((x, y))                    #print a tuple

print("There are <", 2**32, "> possibilities!", sep="*") #
separated by *
```

Get Input data from User

As data can be printed to the standard output (STDOUT), it can also
be taken from user through **the standard input device** which is
usually **the keyboard**. For this the data input is assigned to a
variable using the **input() function** which has an argument as a
prompt message to request information from the user.

```
name = input("Enter your name: ")
print("Hello "+ name)
```

The input is always a string type, so if you try to divide what you get
from input by a number you will get an error. To overcome this,
change the type of variable by converting string to integer with "**int**"
keyword.

```
number = input("Enter number :")
print(int(number)/2)
print(number/2) #=> TypeError: unsupported operand
type(s) for /: 'str' and 'int'
```

READING & WRITING FROM AND TO FILES

To create an empty file open it for writing and then close it.

```
open(file, 'w').close()
```

The **open()** function is a built-in function in module "io" that opens a file for reading, writing or appending input.

```
f = open("c:/new.txt","w")
f.write("Hello World")
f.close()
```

Syntax : open(file, mode='r', buffering=-1, encoding=None, errors=None, newline=None, closefd=True, opener=None)

The input can be text or binary data, in any encoding style. It takes the filename or the path as the first parameter, then which mode you want to use with the file, writing, reading or appending. This is usually a quoted character string: "r" for reading, "w" for writing, and "a" for appending. It defaults to 'rt' which means open for reading in text mode. So, if you want to open a file for reading text only, just use "open(filename)".

The **open()** function returns a stream object which needs to be closed at the end.

Other mode values are 'w' for writing which overwrite the file if it already exists. The 'x' mode implies 'w' and raises an `FileExistsError` to avoid overwriting your files. The 'a' parameter is for appending to the end of the file regardless of the current seek position.

In text mode, if encoding is not specified, the encoding is platform dependent. You may change that by including the parameter for encoding. For reading and writing raw bytes use binary mode and leave encoding unspecified.

The available modes are:

'r' = open for reading (default)

'w' = open for writing, truncating the file first

'x' = create a new file and open it for writing

'a' = open for writing, appending to the end of the file if it exists

'b' = binary mode

't' = text mode (default)

'+' = open a disk file for updating (reading and writing)

```
file = open("d:/new.txt", "a")
seq ="""
\nThis is line 1
\nThis is line 2
\nThis is line 3
"""
file.writelines(seq)
file.close()
```

Python distinguishes between files opened in binary and text modes. Files opened in binary mode (appending 'b' to the mode argument) return contents as **bytes objects** without any decoding. This is useful in some programming operations. If you want to convert it to text mode, encode it first using a specified encoding. Encoding is also used when the contents of a file contains bytes which cannot be displayed on the screen. For example, if the file was saved in Unicode. Another way to overcome, non_ASCII characters is to ignore errors using the flag parameter **"error=ignore"**.

Buffering is an optional integer used to set the buffering policy.

- 0 to switch buffering off (only allowed in binary mode)

- 1 to select line buffering (only usable in text mode)

- integer > 1 to indicate the size of a fixed-size chunk buffer.

Encoding is the name of the encoding model used to decode or encode the file. This should only be used in text mode. The default encoding is platform dependent, but any encoding supported by Python can be passed.

Errors is an optional string that specifies how encoding errors are to be handled

- 'strict' to raise a ValueError exception if there is an encoding error

- the default of None has the same effect

- 'ignore' to ignore errors.(This can lead to data loss).

Newline controls how universal newlines works- it only applies to text mode. It can be None,"",'\n','\r', and '\r\n'". It works as follows:

1. On input, if newline is None, universal newlines mode is enabled.

2. Lines in the input can end in '\n', '\r', or '\r\n' and these are translated into '\n'

3. If it is "", universal newline mode is enabled, but line endings are returned to the caller untranslated.

4. On output, if newline is None, any '\n' characters written are translated to the system default line separator.

5. If newline is " or '\n', no translation takes place.

The open() function returns a file object whose type depends on the mode, and through which the standard file operations such as reading and writing are performed.

```
open("c:/new.txt", "r").read()
```

```
f = open("c:/test.py","r") #f is an object containing the
opened file

string = f.read()          # reading the f object
```

The expression '**with open as'** allow closing the file after operation
is completed.

```
with open("c:/test.txt") as f:
    for line in f:
        print line                    #file closed


    for line in open("c:/test.txt"):
        print line                    #file is still open
```

To open a file by its default executable program use the import the
"os module " and use startfile() function. For example, to open text
files by Microsoft Notepad in Windows use *os.startfile(full path and
name of file)*.

```
import os
os.startfile("c:/py/tut/data/str.txt")
```

RENAMING FILES

To rename a file, you need **the os module** which has a **rename()**
function.

```
import os
os.rename("c:/new.txt", "c:/new.bak")
```

DELETING FILE

To delete a named file use **os module remove() function**.

```
import os
file = "file_name.txt"
os.remove(file)
```

Examining the File Status

If you have a name in a directory, you may need to check its status: is it a file or directory? Does it exist or you need to create it? Is it empty or does it contain some data?

To check if file is empty (zero size):

```
os.path.getsize("c:/test.txt")==0
os.stat("c:/test.txt").st_size==0
```

To check if file actually exists

```
file = "c:/scripts/tut/file.txt"
os.path.exists(file)
```

Is the file empty (zero size)?

```
os.path.getsize("c:/test.txt")
os.stat("c:/test.txt").st_size==0
```

Does the file exist?

```
file = "c:/scripts/tut/file.txt"
os.path.exists(file)
```

Is it a name for file or directory?

The os module has specific functions: **os.path.isfile() and os.path.isdir()**

```
file = "c:\pw.txt"
dir = "c:\py"
```

```
os.path.isfile(file)
os.path.isdir(dir)
```

WORKING WITH DIRECTORIES

How to Create a Directory?

You create (make) a new directory use the **os module**. To avoid errors, check first that the directory does not exist:

```
import os
if not os.path.exists("c:/test"):
    os.mkdir("c:/test")
```

Removing a Directory

To delete a named directory, use the remove directory **"rmdir() "function** in **the os module**:

```
import os
os.rmdir("c:/test")
```

Changing Current Directory

To change working directory to another directory, use the change directory function **"chdir()"** in **the os mod**ule:

```
import os
os.chdir("c:/")
```

If you want to change directory to the current directory where the script is located, use the get current directory function as an argument in the chdir() function.

```
os.chdir(os.getcwd())
```

How to Get the Current Directory Name?

```
import os
os.getcwd()
```

Listing the Directory Content

To list all entries in a directory including both files and folders, us the **"listdir()" function** in os module.

```
os.listdir('c:/py/tut/data')
```

To get a separate list of files, path and directories use **the walk() function** in os module. It walks the tree of directory branches and returns a tuple of three lists:

1. **dirpath:** the path to the directory being walked.

2. **dirnames:** a list of the names of the subdirectories in dirpath

3. **filenames:** a list of the names of the non-directory files in dirpath.

The names in the two lists are just names, with no path components. To get a full path (which begins with the top of tree) use:

```
os.path.join(dirpath, name).
```

Syntax : os.walk = walk(top, topdown=True, onerror=None, followlinks=False)

```
import os
[print(root) for (root, subdirs, files) in os.walk('d:/py')]
[print(subdirs) for (root, subdirs, files) in os.walk('d:/py')]
[print(files) for (root, subdirs, files) in os.walk('d:/py')]
```

Another way to get names of all files with their fullpath is to use the glob module:

```
import glob
glob.glob("d:/**/*") #get all files in a list
```

To list folders only in the directory, use **os.path isdir with glob**:

```
From glob import glob
for d in glob("c:/*/"):
    if os.path.isdir(d):
        print(d)
```

Similarly, to list files only, use **os.path.isfile()** function:

```
from glob import glob
for f in glob("c:/*"):
    if os.path.isfile(f):
        print f
```

It is possible to list files in subdirectories for one or two levels, using glob module:

```
import glob
list = glob.glob("c:/py/*/**")
for i in list:
    if os.path.isdir(i):
        print("Directory: ", i)
    else:
        print "File: ", i
```

To select specific files, you can specify their extension or some characters in their names.

```
import glob
```

```
list = glob.glob("c:/py/*.txt")
list = glob.glob("c:/py/c*t.txt")
list = glob.glob("c:/py/*z?.txt")
```

The **fnmatch() module** can also be used in a similar manner.

```
import fnmatch
for file in os.listdir('c:/py/tut/data/'):
 if fnmatch.fnmatch(file, '*.txt'):
print(file) # print all files with txt extension in data
subfolder
```

Getting the File Stats

The time when the file was accessed, created or modified are written to each file. File size and properties are also included in the file stats. To access this information, you need certain functions from the **os.path** module.

Getting the last time file was accessed

```
fromdatetime import *
at = os.path.getatime("c:/py/tut/data/file.txt")
# 1517755649.4889567
datetime.fromtimestamp(at).strftime('%Y-%m-%d
%H:%M:%S')
#'2018-02-04 14:47:29'
```

Getting the time when the file was created

```
from datetime import *
ct = os.path.getctime("c:/py/tut/data/file.txt") #creation
time
```

```
datetime.fromtimestamp(ct).strftime('%Y-%m-%d
%H:%M:%S'))
```

Getting all the file stats

These include file size, access time, modification time, creation time..etc. (mode, ino, dev, nlink, uid, gid, size, atime, mtime, ctime)

```
os.stat("c:/py/tut/data/file.txt")
```

Getting the file size

To get the file size use os.path module which has a getsize() function.

```
os.path.getsize("c:/scripts/tut/file.txt")
```

How to truncate a file after number of bytes?

```
import os
with open("c:/test.txt", "r+") as f:
f.write("Hello World\nHello World\nHello World")
print os.path.getsize("c:/test.txt")
f.truncate(20)
os.path.getsize("c:/test.txt") open("c:/test.txt", "r").read()
```

Getting the File Path

Certain information about file path and properties may be essential to a programmer. For example, you may need to know:

1. directory path without filename

```
os.path.dirname("c:/scripts/tut/file.txt") #=>
'c:/scripts/tut'
```

2. split path to filename and directory path

```
os.path.split("c:/scripts/tut/file.txt") #=> ('c:/scripts/tut',
'file.txt')
```

3. get extension of filename from its path

```
os.path.splitext("c:/scripts/tut/file.txt")[1]
```

How to get full file path without its extension?

```
import os
os.path.splitext("c:/py/tut/data/file.txt")
#('c:/py/tut/data/file', '.txt')
```

To get full file path without filename

```
import os
os.path.split("c:/py/tut/data/file.txt") #('c:/py/tut/data',
'file.txt')
```

To get file basename from full path

```
from os.path import basename
basename("c:/py/tut/data/file.txt")#=> file.txt
basename("c:/py/tut/data/file.txt")[-3:] #txt
basename("c:/py/tut/data/file.txt")[:-4] #file
join parts of path into full path
os.path.join("c:\script", "tut", "data")
```

DATA

Data Structures

Data structuring is a way of organizing and storing data so that they can be accessed and worked with efficiently. These structures define the relationship between the data, and the operations that can be performed on them. This allow the programmer to concentrate on data operations rather than details of data description and access

Data Structures are divided into two main types:

1. Primitive Data Structures

* **Integers**: These are numbers like 1,2,3,4, etc.

* **Floats:** These are decimal numbers like 12.435

* **Strings:** characters

* **Boolean Value**: which is either True or False.

2. Non-Primitive Data Structures

* **Arrays or Lists:** data containers where data is referenced by index number.

* **Tuples:** fixed lists.

* **Dictionary:** data container where data is referenced by key names.

* **Sets:** fixed list of unique values.

* **Files:** open unindexed data container.

Data Serialization

Data structures may be used in programming by entering them inside the script itself, or entering them each time the script is run from command-line as input by user. When you consider storing them or sending them over a network, you need first to convert them into a stream of bytes. This is called serialization or marshalling.

Data serialization is the process of converting structured data to a format that allows storage of such data, and its retrieval or sharing it across networks in byte streams so that they keep their original structure. In some cases, the secondary intention of data serialization is to reduce the data's size to save the disk space or bandwidth requirements.

Flat or Nested Data

Data can have a flat structure like in the case of a simple list or a dictionary without branching.

```
List = ["one", "two", "three"]
Dictionary = {"name" : "John Smith", "age" : 23, "sex" : male"}
```

Data may also be nested where a key or more in the dictionary will have dictionaries as their values or one or more list element would be lists.

```
Nested = [[1, 2, 3],[4, 5, 6],[7, 8, 9]]
nested_dict = {
'dictA': {'key_1': 'value_1'},
'dictB': {'key_2': 'value_2'}
}


people = {
1: {'name': 'John', 'age': '27', 'sex': 'Male'},
2: {'name': 'Marie', 'age': '22', 'sex': 'Female'}
}
```

Structuring your Data

You need to prepare your data before its serialisation. Data should have a structure to facilitate storage, search and retrieval. It is important to identify or decide how the data should be structured during data serialization - flat or nested. Another decision is which form of serialisation you will use to suit your needs and complexity of your project.

Serializing Text

Simple file (flat data)

The simplest structure for the data to be serialized is locating it in a file like a text file. A text file saved on the hard disk is a source of serialised data structure. It can be retrieved and keep its form when sent over networks. You can think of a text file as a sequence of lines, paragraphs, sentences and words. Each line follows another, and each has a line number (i.e. Index). The text file elements are separated by linefeeds rather than commas in lists. If you give each paragraph a title or heading, the file takes a form of a dictionary with headings as keys and the paragraph as the value of that key. You can then design a code to convert such text file into a dictionary with 'title: subject' pairs for example.

a text file may have a nested structure and contain multiple records similar to a dictionary without quotes or curly brackets:

```
Employee 1:
 Name : Adam Smith
 Age : 25
 Address :2 Somerset Ave., city, UK
Employee 2:
 Name : Simon Alan
 Age : 49
 Address :89 Malcom Lane, city, UK
```

Such structure is found in Windows configuration text files which has the extension ".ini". The structure of **ini** files is based on sections and each section (enclosed in squared brackets) has a number of pairs, each pair on a separate line with key followed by plus = sign before its value.

```
[section]
key1 = value1
key2 = value 2
```

Let's try to create a file containing the following data and name it "example.ini" :

```
[Employee 1]
Name = Adam Smith
Age = 25
Address = 2 Somerset Ave., city, UK
[Employee 2]
Name = Simon Alan
Age= 49
Address = 89 Malcom Lane, city, UK
```

Python has a module to read and write to **'ini' files**. This is the **"Configparser module"**. You can convert data in such 'ini' files into nested dictionaries using the following code with the help of Configparser module. Remember to change "fullpath" to the actual path to the created file.

```
import configparser
parser = configparser.ConfigParser()
parser.read('c:/fullpath/x.ini')
dic = {section: dict(parser.items(section)) for section in
parser.sections()}
print(dic)
```

```
#=>
{
'Employee 1': {'name': 'Adam Smith', 'age': '25', 'address':
'2 Somerset Ave., city, UK'},
'Employee 2': {'name': 'Simon Alan', 'age': '49', 'address':
'89 Malcom Lane, city, UK'}
}
```

It is easy to retrieve data from nested dictionaries. For example, to get the age of employee2.

```
dic["Employee2"]["age"]
```

Notice that all data is returned as strings, so any number needs to be converted to an integer by the keyword **int("number")** first.

CSV file (flat data)

CSV files are also a source of flat data. A CSV File (comma-separated values) is a text file that stores data in the form of columns and rows. Columns are separated by commas, and rows are distinguished by line breaks. It can be imported into Microsoft Excel Spreadsheet software and all other Spreadsheet applications. It has become a universal medium to transfer data between programs and databases. However, it has its limitations when used with a huge amount of data.

Python has a dedicated CSV module to read and write tabular data in CSV format. This module simplifies working with CSV files, although you can read them simply with built-in functions such as **open() and readlines()** as in the following example. Create a csv file and type the following data into it.

```
Name, Age, Sex, Salary
Carol, 23, F, 1200
Adam, 45, M, 3200
```

Then run the following code after changing the fullpath to the right location

```
Employees = open("c:/fullpath/employee.csv").
readlines()

nestedlist=[]

for line in Employees:
    nestedlist.append(line.strip().split(","))

print(nestedlist)

#=> [['Name', ' Age', ' Sex', ' Salary'], ['Carol', ' 23', ' F', '
1200'], ['Adam', ' 45', ' M', ' 3200']]3200]]
```

The CSV module has more functionality. It reads the file after opening it with a **csv.reader(file)** method which return an object(generator) through which you can loop from line to another.

```
import csv

with open("c:/fullpath/em.csv", newline='') as f:
    reader = csv.reader(f)
    for row in reader:
        print(row)

#=>
['Name', ' Age', ' Sex', ' Salary']
['Carol', ' 23', ' F', ' 1200']
['Adam', ' 45', ' M', ' 3200']
```

The module makes writing to CSV file easier, with a **csv.writer(file)** method which returns an object writer. You can feed a list to that writer using the **writerows() method.**

Pickle (nested data)

The native data serialization module for Python is called **Pickle**. Pickle converts data into bytes stream which you can save to a file on the hard disk for later retrieval and use. The byte stream can also be transferred through **ftp** or other internet transfer protocols.

There are mainly two methods in that module: **dump() and load().**

Dump() convert the data into bytes and load() concert them back to their original form. You can save the serialised data bytes into a file.

```
import pickle
grades = { 'Alice': 89, 'Bob': 72, 'Charles': 87 }
pickled = pickle.dumps( grades )
print(pickled)
#=>b'\x80\x04\x95#\x00\x00\x00\x00\x00\x00\x00}\x94(
\x8c\x05Alice\x94KY\x8c\x03Bob\x94KH\x8c\x07Charles\
x94KWu.'
```

Now, the object pickled remains in memory till the session finishes. To save it into a file, you need to open a file **for byte writing**, dump the data into it, and finally close that file. The **dump()** method takes the data object as first parameter and the file object as a second parameter.

```
import pickle
grades = { 'Alice': 89, 'Bob': 72, 'Charles': 87 }
f = open('outfile', 'wb')
pickle.dump(grades, f)
f.close()
```

To retrieve the data, open the file for reading in byte mode and read it and remember to close it.

```
f = open('outfile', 'rb')
unpickled_grades = pickle.load(f)
f.close()
```

```
print(unpickled_grades) #=> {'Alice': 89, 'Bob': 72,
'Charles': 87}
```

Shelve Database

A simple form of a database is a collection of values, where each value is identified by a key and stored in disk. This permanent dictionary is a form of DBM (Database Manager) database. Python has a module in its standard library which save data in permanent dictionary using pickle serialisation. The Shelve module creates a dictionary of pickled Python objects identified by keys and saved to a file as a form of database.

To create a database with Shelve:

```
import shelve
s = shelve,open("db1")
s['name'] = "Ajay"
s['age'] = 23
s['marks'] = 75
s.close()
```

This creates a file named db1 in the current directory and saves the data in hashed form. Later on, you can access the stored data in a dictionary form, by opening the file again:

```
import shelve
s = shelve.open("db1")
print(s['name']) #=> "Ajay"
```

As in any other dictionary, you may use the following functions on the opened shelf object:

1. get(): returns value associated with key

2. items(): list of tuples – each tuple is key value pair in the dictionary.

3. keys(): list of shelve keys

4. pop(): remove specified key and return the corresponding value.

5. update(): Update shelf from another dict/iterable

6. values(): list of shelve values

YAML (nested data)

YAML is essentially a data format for serialisation to parse formatted files into an object which can be written to a file or retrieved back. The main methods in Python PyYaml module is dump() and load() like in Pickle.

To start using YAML in Python you need to install PyYaml module via PIP:

```
pip install pyyaml
```

Yaml files are simply text files with the extension **.yml or .yaml,** and they are formatted according to YAML Syntax.

Data in a yaml file may be flat, like a dictionary or nested like a nested list-dictionary combinations :

```
apples: 20
mangoes: 2
bananas: 3
grapes: 100
pineapples: 1
```

```
sports:
 - soccer
 - football
```

```
 - basketball
 - cricket
 - hockey
 - table tennis
countries:
 - Pakistan
 - USA
 - India
 - China
 - Germany
 - France
 - Spain
```

To read a YAML file we use the **yaml load()** function:

```
import yaml
with open(r'E:\data\fruits.yaml') as file:
    fruits_list = yaml.load(file, Loader=yaml.FullLoader)
```

The **FullLoader** parameter handles the conversion from YAML scalar values to Python dictionary format. Instead of using the FullLoader parameter, you may use **yaml.full_load(file)**to avoid errors in code execution.

To serialize a dictionary and store it into a yaml file format, we use the **dump() function** which take the dictionary object and the filename as parameters.

```
import yaml
dict_file = [{'sports' : ['soccer', 'football', 'basketball',
'cricket', 'hockey', 'table tennis']}],
```

```
{'countries' : ['Pakistan', 'USA', 'India', 'China', 'Germany',
'France', 'Spain']}]

with open(r'E:\data\store_file.yaml', 'w') as file:

    documents = yaml.dump(dict_file, file)
```

To sort keys in your file, use sort_keys=True

```
sort_file = yaml.dump(doc, sort_keys=True)
```

YAML SYNTAX

* the file should end in **.yaml**

* Yaml document starts with 3 dashes "- - -" and ends with 3 dots
"..."

* Yaml is case sensitive

* Do not use tabs

* Scalars are the data values: strings, integers, floats or a Boolean.

* Scalars are unquoted, but quote them if they confuse the parser.

* Sequence is a list of items on the same level indicated by a space
and a dash -.

* Sequence can be nested, each branch moved one space to the right.

* Comments are indicated by initial #

* A block of scalar data may have linefeeds preserved if you follow
the colon with | after the compulsory space

```
include_newlines: |

exactly as you see

will appear these three

lines of poetry
```

: > will fold linefeeds into spaces

* Any string containing the following characters should be quoted to avoid syntax errors:

```
[] {} > | * & ! % # ` @ ,.
```

* Data is structured in lists and dictionaries:

* A list can be represented by:

```
- Apple
- Orange
- Strawberry
- Mango
```

or

```
['Apple', 'Orange', 'Strawberry', 'Mango']
```

* A dictionary can be represented as:

```
- martin:
- name: Martin Developer
- job: Developer
- skill: Elite
```

* A complex structure includes both lists and dictionaries:

```
# Employee records
- martin:
  name: Martin D'vloper
  job: Developer
  skills:
```

```
    - python
    - perl
    - pascal
- tabitha:
  name: Tabitha Bitumen
  job: Developer
  skills:
    - lisp
    - fortran
    - erlang
```

JSON file (nested data)

JSON is a data file format to transfer, storing and exchange of data. JSON stands for "JavaScript Object Notation". It uses **key:value** pairs (Dictionaries) and lists (Arrays) to structure data.

```
{"firstName": "John",
"lastName": "Smith",
"isAlive": true,
"age": 27,
"address": {
  "streetAddress": "21 2nd Street",
  "city": "New York",
  "state": "NY",
  "postalCode": "10021-3100"
},
"phoneNumbers": [
```

```
{
  "type": "home",
  "number": "212 555-1234"
},
{
  "type": "office",
  "number": "646 555-4567"
}
],
"children": [],
"spouse": null
}
```

Python's JSON module can be used to read and write JSON files. To convert data type to json use the **loads() function** in json module:

```
import json
x ='{ "name":"John", "age":30, "city":"New York"}'
y = json.loads(x)
```

The folllowing objects can be converted using the json module:

- dict

- list

- tuple

- string

- int

- float

- True

- False

- None

To display json data we use the **dumps() function** in json module:

```
import json
json.dumps(x)
```

To make the output more readable, dumps() takes two parameters: one for indentation and the other for separators:

json.dumps(x, indent=4)

```
{
 "name": "John",
 "age": 30,
 "married": true,
 "divorced": false,
 "children": [
"Ann",
"Billy"
],
 "pets": null,
 "cars": [
{
"model": "BMW 230",
"mpg": 27.5
},
{
"model": "Ford Edge",
"mpg": 24.1
```

```
        }
    ]
}
```

json.dumps(x, indent=4, separators=(". ", " = "))

```
{
    "name" = "John".
    "age" = 30.
    "married" = true.
    "divorced" = false.
    "children" = [
"Ann".
"Billy"
    ].
    "pets" = null.
    "cars" = [
{
"model" = "BMW 230".
"mpg" = 27.5
}.
{
"model" = "Ford Edge".
"mpg" = 24.1
}
    ]
}
```

You can also sort keys of dictionaries:

json.dumps(x, indent=4, sort_keys=True)

```
{
 "age": 30,
 "cars": [
{
"model": "BMW 230",
"mpg": 27.5
},
{
"model": "Ford Edge",
"mpg": 24.1
}
],
 "children": [
"Ann",
"Billy"
],
 "divorced": false,
 "married": true,
 "name": "John",
 "pets": null
}
```

To read a json file, open the file and load its contents:

```
import json
with open('/tmp/file.json', 'r') as f:
```

```
data = json.load(f)
```

To write data to json file, open file and dump the data into it:

```
import json
with open('/tmp/file.json', 'w') as f:
    json.dump(data, f, sort_keys=True)
```

XML (nested data)

The Extensible Markup Language (XML) is a text-encoding language much like HTML or SGML which is the language used on web pages as a standard. It is extremely useful for storage of small to medium amounts of data without requiring a database. It is based on a set of rules for organising data in documents that is both human-readable and machine-readable.

XML parsing in Python is possible using the xml package, which has XML handling submodules. These are very useful for scraping and crawling information from the internet through **APIs** (Application Programming Interface).

One of these submodules is **"xml.etree.ElementTree.**

The **ElementTree API** is a simple and lightweight XML processor. It provides a simple and efficient API for parsing and creating XML data. XML is a hierarchical data format, and the most natural way to represent it is with a tree. The **ElementTree (ET) API** has two classes to interact with such tree:

1- **ElementTree** represents the whole tree and

2- **Element Class** to represent a single node in that tree.

ElementTree is used to interact with the whole XML document file. For example, here is XML example in Python which organise data about three countries. Copy it into a file with extension ".xml" in the same directory, e.g. 'country_data.xml'

```xml
<?xml version="1.0"?>
<data>
  <country name="Liechtenstein">
    <rank>1</rank>
    <year>2008</year>
    <gdppc>141100</gdppc>
    <neighbor name="Austria" direction="E"/>
    <neighbor name="Switzerland" direction="W"/>
  </country>
  <country name="Singapore">
    <rank>4</rank>
    <year>2011</year>
    <gdppc>59900</gdppc>
    <neighbor name="Malaysia" direction="N"/>
  </country>
  <country name="Panama">
    <rank>68</rank>
    <year>2011</year>
    <gdppc>13600</gdppc>
    <neighbor name="Costa Rica" direction="W"/>
    <neighbor name="Colombia" direction="E"/>
  </country>
</data>
</xml>
```

You can get the whole tree from the xml file using the following code:

```
import xml.etree.ElementTree as ET
tree = ET.parse('country_data.xml')
root = tree.getroot()
```

The tree contains elements organised as nodes one after another.

Each element in the tree has a tag and attributes. So, the root has its tag 'data' but has no attribute. Each child element has tag 'country' and attributes. To get the data in these child elements, we use tag() and attrib() functions:

```
for child in root:
    print(child.tag, child.attrib)
#=>
country {'name': 'Liechtenstein'}
country {'name': 'Singapore'}
country {'name': 'Panama'}
```

You can access a specific node data by its index if you know its position and get its text by the **text method** as the tree is similar to a nested list of items:

```
import xml.etree.ElementTree as ET
tree = ET.parse("country.xml")
root = tree.getroot()
print(root[0][1].text) #=> 2008 first node second item
(year)
```

If the xml data is in a text file with extension "txt", you still can get the tree from that long string with the method **ET.fromstring(text):**

```
data_string = open("xml.txt", 'r').read()
root = ET.fromstring(data_string)
root[0][1].text #=> 2008
```

A better way to access data in the xml tree is to use **Element class methods**. **Element.iter(tag)** class iterate over all the children of the tree recursively and return its nodes which has a tag matching the tag given. In the following example we are getting each *neighbor* of each country *node*:

```
import xml.etree.ElementTree as ET
tree = ET.parse("country.xml")
root = tree.getroot()
for neighbor in root.iter('neighbor'):
    print(neighbor.attrib)
#=>
 {'name': 'Austria', 'direction': 'E'}
 {'name': 'Switzerland', 'direction': 'W'}
 {'name': 'Malaysia', 'direction': 'N'}
 {'name': 'Costa Rica', 'direction': 'W'}
 {'name': 'Colombia', 'direction': 'E'}
```

Element.findall(tag) will find all elements with such a tag that are children of the current element. Then you can get all sub-children data using the right tag and attribute methods: **find()** to get the first tag and **get()** to get the attribute of that node. For example, to get all the ranks of each country:

```
import xml.etree.ElementTree as ET
tree = ET.parse("country.xml")
root = tree.getroot()
for country in root.findall('country'): #for each country in
the root tree
```

```
    rank = country.find('rank').text     #find rank
    name = country.get('name')           #get name
    print(name, rank))
#=>
Liechtenstein 1
Singapore 4
Panama 68
```

XPATH

XPath is an expression language that allows the processing of values conforming to the data model defined in the XQuery and Xpath Data Model. You can search the XML tree using XPATH syntax. Python XML package support a *limited set of expressions* used in XPATH. The following are the supported XPath Expressions:

tag = Selects all child elements with the given tag.

{namespace}* = selects all tags in the given namespace

{}* = only selects tags that are not in a namespace.

* = Selects all child elements, including comments and processing instructions.

\. = Selects the current node. This is mostly useful at the beginning of the path.

**** = Selects all sub elements, on all levels beneath the current element.

.. = Selects the parent element.

[@attrib] = Selects all elements that have the given attribute.

[@attrib='value'] = Selects all elements for which the given attribute has the given value. The value cannot contain quotes.

[tag] = Selects all elements that have a child named tag. Only immediate children are supported.

[.='text'] = Selects all elements whose complete text content, including descendants, equals the given text.

[tag='text'] = Selects all elements that have a child named tag, whose complete text content, including descendants, equals the given text.

[position] = Selects all elements that are located at the given position.

Predicates (expressions within square brackets) = must be preceded by a tag name, an asterisk, or another predicate. **position predicates** must be preceded by a tag name

```
import xml.etree.ElementTree as ET

tree = ET.parse("country.xml")

root = tree.getroot()

years = root.findall(".//year")

for year in years:

    print(year.text)

#=>

2008

2011

2011

[print(i.text) for i in root.findall('.//*rank')]

#=>

1

4

68
```

DOCUMENTATION

Documenting while Coding

It is a matter of good practice to document you script while coding. This makes it more readable and useable. Readers and developers will be able to understand what is your plan and what is the structure of your design? What are the different parts of the code about? and What do you expect to get out of each line of code?

Comments

The simplest form of documenting is adding comments to the code. Comments are ignored by the interpreter as any part of the code line anywhere that comes after "#". Comments are mainly used for short remarks and run only for one line. You may use multiline comments if you add the "#" sign at the start of each line.

Comments are used for multiple purposes:

1. Planning you code: overall design

2. Sectioning your code to different integrated parts.

3. Description of the purpose of each section.

4. Tagging areas of you code which needs revision for bugs, errors, improvement or future updating (things to TODO, things to fix, as a reminder, bugs you intend to remove or correct.

The design of code in itself would make it readable and easier to understand if you use meaningful names for classes, functions and variables which are self-explanatory, and are based on their action or purpose.

Docstrings

Docstrings are the extensive strings you add to your code to explain everything about it to the users, developers and even yourself reading it later. Every module or python file should have this form of documentation. Python has a functions to retrieve, format, display it on the console or write this documentation to a file.

Docstrings use the triple-quote string format """ABC""". It may be a single line string, or multiline paragraphs. If it is multiline docstring, it should consist of 4 parts:

1. Summary Line

2. Blank Line

3. Details on multilines

4. Blank Line

Class docstrings are added just below class definition and each method definition line. They should be indented. Module docstrings are similar, although sometimes a general docstring is placed at the top of the module, before any other statement or imports. In a package, they are placed at the top of the __init__.py file in the package folder.

When a script of code is run from the console, it contains its parameters (arguments) or the user is asked to enter some parameters on the console. Command-line parameters are used to interact with these scripts. There are two ways to input parameters to a script:

1. **sys.argv[1:]** : This is a list of command-line arguments passed to the Python program.

2. **argparse module arguments**

In the case of scripts which has **argparse** arguments, the description parameter takes __doc__ which displays the docstring at the top of script whenever the user run the script-name on the console with -h parameter. This usually includes instructions to the user on how to use the script and various optional parameters.

The help() utility

Python has a help utility which display documentation on console for :

1. modules

2. keywords

3. symbols

4. topics

5. operators

6. builtins objects

7. modules in standard library

8. third-party packages

After you enter interactive mode on Python (by typing Python on command-line), type **help** to get into **help interactive mode**. While at help prompt, enter:

1. module: to get a list of all installed modules.

2. keywords: to get a list of all keywords.

3. symbols: to get a list of all Python symbols.

4. topics: to get a list of documentation topics.

if you type **help(topic)** you will get a summary on that particular topic. To search for a module on the help prompt, type (pattern). This will return a list of modules who has that pattern in their name or summary.

The pydoc Module

Python include a module in its standard library which generate documentation for modules in formatted pages which can be displayed on the console or saved to file. It derives the documentation from the docstrings of the module or package, or from comments if no docstring is available.

The **help()** built-in function invokes the help interactive system which uses the pydoc module to prepare its text documentation.

You can invoke the display of documentation for any module, keyword or topic by typing the following on the console prompt:

```
python -m pydoc <topic)
```

To save this documentation to a text file in current directory, use:

```
python -m pydoc <topic> > filename.txt
```

To save the documentation as an html file in the current directory use:

```
python -m pydoc -w sys #=> wrote sys.html
```

To get a list of all modules:

```
python -c help('modules')
```

To get a list of all builtins, get to Python shell by typing Python at the CMD prompt and then type:

```
dir(__builtins__)
```

This will return a list of all builtins.

Documentation online

The official Python documentation can be found online. There are also a number of good tutorials. There is a big library of books to learn Python such as:

1. Python Cookbook: Recipes for Mastering Python 3

2. Python Pocket Reference: Python in Your Pocket

3. Learn Python the Hard Way

DESIGN

How to Design and Plan your Python Programming Project?

Before you start writing your Python code and test it, it is very important to step back and think about your project plan and how to design it before putting down any single statement.

What do you want to make?

First, think about the purpose of your program, what do you want to make? What purpose would it serve? Give it a clear description. Think about explaining it to someone in a single paragraph.

The description will summarize the components and interactions within the program. For example, let us say we want to develop a Quiz Program: we can describe it as:

"An interactive test application using saved multiple answer questions which are displayed on screen one by one and the user will answer by selecting one answer only. If his answer is correct it will be added to his total score which will be displayed at the end of program"

What are the features of your project?

The second step is to decide on the features of your project and how it will look like. To clarify things visually, you may write down a sketch of your program components and how they interact together. The main components of any program are:

```
input ---> Processing ---> output
```

Input:

1. MCQs –> get from Saved file.

2. User answer –> get from keyboard input.

Output:

1. MCQs –> display one by one on screen (may be time-limited)

2. Message to user to select answer.

3. Total score at the end.

Processing :

1. Read the saved MCQs file

2. Display MCQs one by one and wait for answer.

3. Ask user to select one answer.

4. Get the user answer.

5. Compare answer to stored correct answers.

6. Add score if answer is correct.

7. Repeat until all MCQs are used.

8. Display message with total score and Advice

How to carry the plan out?

Think of Python code as a collection of objects, data, user interactions, and logic. In the above example, there are a number of objects:

1. File that contains MCQs and Answers: –> it can take the form of data object as *dictionary* of "question: answer" pairs.

2. Display output: print to screen

3. User Input: integer added to a count sum.

4. Compare input to dictionary value.

5. Calculation: add 1 score or none to total score.

What is the structure of your project?

Now, it is the time to think of the structure of your project in more details, in the form of files, modules, classes, functions and data. The above details would definitely help.

* Prepare the questions in a **json file** with an MCQ as a key and correct answer as a value.

```
{
" A string in Python can be quoted by : \n 1-Single quote\n 2-Double Quote\n 3-Triple Quote \n 4-All of above. ": "4",

"A list is a sequence of : \n 1-Integers\n 2-Strings \n 3-Any Object \n 4-dictionaries" : "3"
}
```

* An alternative is to use a text file and convert its content into a dictionary. for example:

```
A String object must have :
  1- Double Quotes
  2- Single Quotes
  3- Triple quotes
  4- All of the above
As: 4
A list is a sequence of :
  1- Integers
  2- Strings
  3- Any object
  4- None of the above
As: 3
```

This file content can be converted into a dictionary using this code:

```
dic = {}
content = open("try.txt", 'r').read()
conlist = content.split("\n\n")
for item in conlist:
    parts = item.split("As:")
dic[parts[0]] = parts[1].strip()
```

This gives the following dictionary:

```
dic #=> {
"A String object must have :\n 1- Double Quotes\n 2-
Single Quotes\n 3- Triple quotes\n 4- All of the above\n":
"4",
"A list is a sequence of :\n 1- Integers\n 2- Strings\n 3-
Any object\n 4- None of the above\n": "3"
}
#IMPORTANT : keys should have double quotes not single
quotes
```

1. Function: Read questions from file – Load json file into a dictionary.

2. Function: display keys of "MCQs" on screen one by one – use **print**.

3. Function: Ask user to select an number and wait – use **Input**.

4. Get the input, convert to integer.

5. Compare the user response to value of that MCQ answer using "If " and "==".

6. Add one to total score if answer is correct using: total score += 1.

7. Repeat for rest of questions – Loop.

8. Display total score and advice – use **print**.

Here is the complete script of the quiz project. It is also available to download here.:

```python
class Quiz():
    def __init__(self, score = 0):
        "initialize the score value"
    self.score = score

    def Read_mcqas(self):
        "read the json file containing MCQs and answers in
key:value pairs and return a dictionary"
        import json
        global mcas
        with open("MCQs.json", 'r') as f:
            mcas = json.load(f)
            return mcas
    def Display_MCQs(self):
        "Display each MCQ and get answer, compare to value
and add to score"
        mcqs = self.Read_mcqas()
        for mcq in mcqs:
            print(mcq)
            ans = input("Select number of correct answer: ")
            if ans == mcqs[mcq]:
```

```
        self.score += 1
      self.Result()
    def Result(self):
      "display result and advice"
      print("Here is the total score ...:", self.score)
      print("This is a percentage of ...",
(self.score/len(mcas))*100, "%")


m = Quiz()
print(m.Display_MCQs())
```

The Internet Radio Project

Here is another script to develop an Internet Radio to play a number of radio stations online.

Purpose : Listen to online radio stations.

Required :

1. **A list of (urls) links** of online radio stations. For example, for stations broadcasting classic music:

stations = {"Mozart": "http://listen.shoutcast.com/radio-mozart",

"ClassicFM":"http://media-ice.musicradio.com/ClassicFMMP3"}

2. A **music player** . For example, download "**mplayer**" for Windows from the internet and install it.

Sections of script :

1. List stations on console

2. User to select a station.

3. Play station

List Stations

The **urls** can be put in a dictionary in the same script file or in a separate file. It is possible to print their keys (station names) using enumerate built-in function with index as a number (starting with 1) for the user to select his favourite station later on:

```python
def list_stations():
    print("Welcome to Internet Radio")
    print("Stations are:\n"+"="*70)
    for index, station in enumerate(stations, 1):
        print("{:<5}{: <10}".format(index, station))
```

Select Station

This function will call the previous one, to list the numbered station names. Then ask the user to select a number, then convert this selected number into an integer while making it global variable to be accessed outside this function. Then the next function will play this station through the next function.

```python
def station_selector():
    list_stations()
    print("="*70)
    selected = input("Please enter the number of the
station you want.\n or <ENTER> to 'quit' \n ")
    if selected :
        global station_index
        station_index = int(selected)
        play_station()
    else:
```

exit

Play Station

In this function we want to play station and display what is being played now.

Here we want to run "mplayer.exe" with the **url** selected as an argument.

We get the url from the stations dictionary by getting the name of the station from the index selected by user. we deduct 1 from that index as indices start with 0 and we started numbers with 1.

```
url = stations[list(stations.keys())[station_index-1]]
import os

def play_station():
    url = stations[list(stations.keys())[station_index-1]]
os.system("c:/mplayer/mplayer.exe",url")
```

Learning Points

1. Use of dictionary and calling its keys and values

2. Display a list on screen using enumerate function.

3. Formatting output using format function.

4. Using input function to get user selection.

The Complete Script:

The complete script can be downloaded Python/radio.py at master · Sabryfattah/Python · GitHub

How to improve your coding skills?

Python is an incredibly powerful and versatile programming language. It has become one of the most popular languages in the world and is used for a variety of applications. If you're looking to improve your programming skills in Python, there are a few key steps you can take.

This book helps you in the first steps to improve your programming skills in Python through learning the basics. This included understanding the syntax, data types, and basic control structures. You should also become familiar with the standard library and the most common third-party packages.

Practice Regularly

The best way to improve coding skills is to design and test more simple programs and correct your mistakes and errors. Programming is a skill that is learnt through practice.

Reading scripts and programs written by others is another way to learn and get more ideas. There are thousands of programs written in python which you can download for free on Python Package Index (https://pypi.org/). This is a repository of programming projects uploaded by the programming community and it has currently 425,545 projects. Another source is (https://github.com/python) where Python projects are uploaded.

Before you start your own project, search these repositories for a similar project. Most likely, someone has written a similar code. Read through it and make modifications that suits your needs. Trying and testing others' projects and making some modifications in the code is the best way to improve your coding skills. You will discover new techniques and ingenious ideas for achieving what you aim for. If you find something you cannot fully understand, read about it online. There are sites such as (https://stackoverflow.com/) where you find answers to your questions or ask the programming community to help you solve your problem.

You do not need to build a programming project from scratch, many projects need to import modules from other projects. You can install any project in Python Package Index into your computer and use it in your program as a source for imported modules. **pip** is the package installer that is already available in Python. You can use **pip** to install packages from the Python Package Index and other indexes. Just type **pip install <name pf package>** and it will be installed into your third part packages in Python location on your computer.

When starting to use a new package, work through its tutorials and documentations. To get a list of all modules installed in Python on your computer, type this on the console:

```
python -c help('modules')
```

To get documentation on any installed module, function or class, use the following:

```
python -m pydoc <module name>
```

Taking part in coding challenges allows developing skills in steps with the stimulation of feedback about your strengths and weaknesses. Search for coding challenges sites online and choose what suits your level of skills.

Creating small projects is the best way to feel mastery on your programming competence. The more you practice, the better you'll become a master at problem-solving and writing efficient code.

Python is constantly evolving, so it's important to keep up with the latest developments. This includes reading blogs and articles, attending conferences, and watching tutorials and talks. This will help you stay up-to-date on the latest trends and best practices.

The Python community is very active and welcoming. You can get involved by attending local meetups, participating in online forums and Q&A sites, and contributing to open-source projects. This is a great way to learn from experienced developers and get feedback on your code.

One of the best ways to improve your programming skills in Python is to automate tasks. This can be done by writing scripts to automate repetitive tasks, such as downloading files, creating reports, and running tests. This is also a great way to practice your coding skills and become more efficient.

If you want to develop web applications, you should learn a web framework such as Django or Flask. These frameworks make it easier to build web applications by providing a set of tools and libraries. They also make it easier to deploy your applications to a web server.

If you want to develop graphical user interfaces, you should learn a GUI toolkit such as Tkinter or PyQt. These toolkits make it easier to create graphical interfaces with buttons, menus, and other widgets.

If you still feel in need of more knowledge and practice, taking an online course is one of the best ways to improve your programming skills in Python. There are a variety of courses available, ranging from introductory courses to more advanced topics. This is a great way to learn from experienced instructors and get feedback on your code.

Finally, reading books is a great way to improve your programming skills in Python. There are a variety of books available, ranging from introductory books to more advanced topics. This is a great way to learn from experienced authors and get a deeper understanding of the language.

Improving your programming skills in Python takes time and effort, but it's well worth it. By following the above steps, you can become a better programmer and open up a world of possibilities.

Contents